S0-EAS-644

NEW DIRECTIONS FOR COMMUNITY COLLEGES

Arthur M. Cohen
EDITOR-IN-CHIEF

Florence B. Brawer
ASSOCIATE EDITOR

Paula Zeszotarski
PUBLICATION COORDINATOR

Building Successful Relationships Between Community Colleges and the Media

Clifton Truman Daniel
Janel Henriksen Hastings
Harry S Truman College

EDITORS

Number 110, Summer 2000

JOSSEY-BASS
San Francisco

Clearinghouse for Community Colleges

BUILDING SUCCESSFUL RELATIONSHIPS BETWEEN COMMUNITY COLLEGES AND THE MEDIA
Clifton Truman Daniel, Janel Henriksen Hastings (eds.)
New Directions for Community Colleges, no. 110
Volume XXVIII, number 2
Arthur M. Cohen, Editor-in-Chief; Florence B. Brawer, Associate Editor

This issue is dedicated to the memory of E. Clifton Daniel Jr., former managing editor of the New York Times

New Directions for Community Colleges is indexed in Current Index to Journals in Education (ERIC).

Microfilm copies of issues and articles are available in 16mm and 35mm, as well as microfiche in 105mm, through University Microfilms Inc., 300 North Zeeb Road, Ann Arbor, Michigan 48106-1346.

ISSN 0194-3081   ISBN 0-7879-5427-6

NEW DIRECTIONS FOR COMMUNITY COLLEGES is part of The Jossey-Bass Higher and Adult Education Series and is published quarterly by Jossey-Bass Inc., 350 Sansome Street, San Francisco, California 94104-1342, in association with the ERIC Clearinghouse for Community Colleges. Periodicals postage paid at San Francisco, California, and at additional mailing offices. POSTMASTER: Send address changes to New Directions for Community Colleges, Jossey-Bass Inc., 350 Sansome Street, San Francisco, California 94104-1342.

SUBSCRIPTIONS cost $60.00 for individuals and $107.00 for institutions, agencies, and libraries. Prices subject to change.

THE MATERIAL in this publication is based on work sponsored wholly or in part by the Office of Educational Research and Improvement, U.S. Department of Education, under contract number ED-99-CO-0010. Its contents do not necessarily reflect the views of the Department or any other agency of the U.S. Government.

EDITORIAL CORRESPONDENCE should be sent to the Editor-in-Chief, Arthur M. Cohen, at the ERIC Clearinghouse for Community Colleges, University of California, 3051 Moore Hall, Box 951521, Los Angeles, California 90095-1521. All manuscripts receive anonymous reviews by external referees.

Cover photograph © Rene Sheret, After Image, Los Angeles, California, 1990.

Printed in the United States of America on acid-free recycled paper containing 100 percent recovered waste paper, of which at least 20 percent is postconsumer waste.

CONTENTS

Editors' Notes

Community college students throughout the United States represent the largest segment of students in American higher education. To date, approximately 10.4 million students are enrolled in two-year colleges, making up 45 percent of all undergraduate students in America. Although community colleges play an increasingly important role in the lives of millions of Americans, they have difficulty establishing and maintaining visibility within their communities, and keeping students and potential business and industry partners aware of and interested in their programs. One solution to this dilemma may be related to the manner in which colleges promote and market their academic programs and services throughout their surrounding communities.

In the face of limited budgets allocated for institutional advancement, it is important that community college practitioners turn to one particular resource that can be invaluable for promoting a college's academic programs and services: *the media*. To market community colleges as a viable resource for college-level education and workforce and career development, marketing and public relations departments can forge strong communication links with local media outlets, including newspapers and radio and television stations. The task, of course, is understanding how best to create these working relationships in a manner that is effective and beneficial for both college and media representatives.

The objective of this volume is to describe current relationships between two-year colleges and the media across the country. The chapters in this volume will address three themes: (1) the history of community colleges' relationships with members of the press; (2) the media's relationships with community college practitioners; and (3) strategic college marketing through media outlets. As a whole, this volume relates a very important message: the need to ensure that community colleges are visible to the community and that their mission and purpose are widely known. Of particular significance is the recurring theme that is mentioned by the authors contributing to this volume; that is, the importance of establishing positive relationships between community college leaders and members of the press.

A review of current research in the community college arena reveals little about the best practices for working with the media for the purpose of institutional advancement. Likewise, information is limited regarding how members of the press view and operationalize their working relationships with educators. It is our goal to provide a starting point for future discussions on this important topic, and to prompt educators and members of the press corps alike to reevaluate their current and future work with each other. This volume introduces practical strategies—from the vantage point of community college leaders, consultants, and media professionals—that all parties can use to advance their institutions' visibility and to create lasting relationships with the press.

The chapters in this volume represent opinions from both sides of the fence that separates public relations people from members of the media, and it helps to remember that both camps are wary of each other. Journalists say, only partly in jest, that when a member of the press corps jumps the fence to work in public relations, he or she is "going over to the dark side." Public relations professionals, on the other hand, sometimes regard journalists as underpaid, overworked "guttersnipes"—as President Harry S Truman once referred to one of them—who are hot for scandal and nothing else.

While the vast majority of professionals on both sides are honest and straightforward in their dealings, it pays to remember that we are, after all, advocating the building of relationships. And relationships, though they are the very things that make it a joy to be human, are seldom easy and uncomplicated. The best advice, therefore, is to take all this in and then do what works best for you.

As noted, this volume is organized into three key areas. In the first chapter, Janel Hastings explores early examples of how the media have been utilized by educational institutions for the purposes of marketing and publicity. The manner in which community colleges and the press have been "perceived" by each other is also explored.

Current examples of effective relationships between the media and colleges begin with Clifton Truman Daniel's contribution. Here, Daniel identifies open and consistent communication as the key element in creating lasting and positive relationships between colleges and the media representatives.

Neal A. Raisman, a private consultant, provides practical suggestions and procedures for establishing beneficial interactions with members of the press.

Tim Thornton, of the *Greensboro News and Record,* provides ideas about what the press really needs from community college leaders, educators, and administrators to market current and future programs through a process that is logical and time-efficient, and meets the needs of all parties.

Anthony Marquez, of the Associated Press, provides further suggestions and advice on how colleges can promote their programs and services in ways that will receive positive feedback and notice from news journalists.

In considering methods to use in incorporating the media into colleges' strategic marketing campaigns, Mark L. Wallace offers ideas—from the vantage point of a seasoned public relations professional—on how colleges can use media resources to advertise academic programs, workforce training, and continuing education opportunities.

Janel Hastings describes how a current project at one of the City Colleges of Chicago campuses succeeded in using statistical data and marketing strategies to improve the college's visibility through popular media outlets.

Lucy Lee discusses the extent to which journalists and community college practitioners can collaborate to improve the public image of community colleges, as well as to enhance and augment administrators' and college faculty members' ability to improve the curriculum.

The final section of this edition focuses on the future of college-media relations and the influence of the Web on colleges' ability to achieve institutional advancement. Christine Tatum looks at how the Internet can be used to give students course credit and real-world media experience within community college journalism programs. Clifton Daniel then provides suggestions and tips on "etiquette" when using the Internet as a means of institutional promotion.

Clifton Truman Daniel
Janel Henriksen Hastings
Editors

CLIFTON TRUMAN DANIEL *is director of public relations at Harry S Truman College, one of the City Colleges of Chicago. He worked for fifteen years as a feature writer and editor with the* Morning Staff *in Wilmington, North Carolina.*

JANEL HENRIKSEN HASTINGS *is the assistant dean of research and planning at Harry S Truman College, one of the City Colleges of Chicago. She worked for two years with the Center for the Study of Community Colleges and the ERIC Clearinghouse at the University of California, Los Angeles.*

1

This chapter discusses the media's historical role in helping community colleges define and market their individual and collective identity as institutions of higher education.

Community Colleges and the Media: Defining Identity

Janel Henriksen Hastings

Edmund Gleazer (1994) said it best in his foreword to *America's Community Colleges: The First Century:* "We are not well understood" (p. vii). It has long been the challenge of community colleges throughout the nation to create for themselves an identity that reflects both the unique qualities that define a two-year college education and an identity that complements community colleges' contribution to the system of modern higher education. Gleazer, president emeritus of the American Association of Community Colleges, correctly noted that "there is in community college history a discernible search for institutional identity, that is, for recognition and public understanding in terms of a mission different from . . . [and] similar to the missions of . . . the secondary school and the college" (p. vii).

The issue of public perception of the community college has been addressed, among other ways, by a cavalcade of marketing and public relations efforts at local, state, and national levels. Some are modest and some are elaborate (Cohen and Brawer, 1996), but the ultimate goal of these publicity campaigns is to ensure that community colleges' public constituents are aware of the programs, services, and educational opportunities available at their local college campus.

To do this, of course, requires that college administrators understand clearly and be very familiar with the public and corporate resources available to the community college if they are to disseminate a college's mission and objectives. Near the top of the long list of potential allies in this endeavor are the *media.*

Newspapers, radio, and television outlets have played an active role in helping institutions of higher education advertise their services to a widely diverse market of potential and current students. This chapter will review the media's role in helping community colleges take an active lead in augmenting and improving their public visibility, and disseminating to the public their identity as a system of higher education.

Establishing Identity

A review of literature focusing on the media's historical role in the development and growth of community colleges turns up very little data. A very real phenomenon surrounds the modern perception of the two-year college; that is, by reputation, word of mouth, or media coverage, community colleges have survived despite the negative identifications attached to them. This is illustrated through the work of La Paglia (1994), who looked at the identity of community colleges through a different mode of written communication: American fiction and women's personal journals. In *Storytellers: The Image of the Two-Year College in American Fiction and in Women's Journals,* La Paglia sought answers to key questions, including: (1) what is the image of the two-year college, why is there a scarcity of references to two-year college people, and why the usual belittling depiction when they do appear? and (2) what effect does the negative image have on two-year college students or prospective students, are two-year college students and faculty members even aware of the popular negative conceptions, and does this perception keep the people who need community college the most from enrolling? (La Paglia, 1994).

The average community college student, as depicted in the novels and personal diaries La Paglia studied, is white, middle-class, and female, and is reentering school part-time after a long absence. La Paglia noted that between 1970 and 1980 community college students were rarely portrayed as central characters in fictional works. The portrayal of the community college student changed in the 1990s, with the white, middle-class female no longer being representative of this student demographic. The portrayal of community college faculty members has been similar: the average two-year college faculty member is a white, male English instructor, whose teaching role is merely incidental, if not irrelevant, to the character's main activities.

La Paglia (1994) compared these fictional representations of community college faculty and students with actual writings produced by female two-year college students and their instructors. In direct contrast to the fictional representation of community college students, La Paglia found these students to be active in planning their own lives and saw that they recognized and resented their marginal status within higher education and enjoyed learning in an educational setting that was, for many of them, a haven. And she saw that faculty members, as opposed to their depiction in books and on television, constantly focused on their sense of mission, educated themselves throughout their careers, and were aware of the perceived and actual marginality of their students.

A limited number of literature citations regarding community colleges' relationships with the media concern the difficulty the media has had in capturing and advertising not only the mission but also the *identity* of a community college. For example, Sicking and Harris (1976) conducted an analysis of press coverage given to the Metropolitan Junior College District in Kansas City, Missouri, between 1965 and 1975. The authors found that while community colleges provide a wide range of services and programs to a student population whose personal and professional needs are constantly changing, the complex nature of community colleges' services makes their identity less tangible and understandable to the community at large. The authors' 1975 survey of community constituents found that "most people in the district [knew] little or nothing about the community college system, . . . thus highlighting the existence of an identity problem within the two-year college system." The authors noted that "this lack of a clearly defined identity is more difficult to understand with the realization that . . . the junior college system from which the community college district developed has been part of the educational picture since 1915" (1976, p. 9).

Sicking and Harris's study also highlights two key problem areas that hinder professional journalists' ability to provide news coverage within the education arena: the journalistic weakness for emphasizing trouble rather than achievement, and school and college administrators' inherent resistance to allowing criticism to "go public." The data collected by the authors regarding community college news coverage between 1965 and 1975 indicate a sharp decline in the number of articles and press releases printed during this ten-year period and highlight the fact that while the colleges may have had press coverage, the type of coverage they have received has often been inadequate to "establish in the minds of the readers . . . a positive identification of the college, its goals and objectives" (1976, p. 15).

Marketing Identity

To be sure, community colleges have relied on the media as a venue for advertising current and newsworthy events on campus. Still, the history of the relationships between the media and colleges is not well documented. At best, historical literature suggests that the media—including radio, television, and newspaper—have traditionally been among many players in larger, institution- or district-wide marketing campaigns developed by colleges and districts nationwide. Certainly, the media have been instrumental in helping community colleges advertise a campus identity to a large community constituency. The problem remains, however, in understanding how community colleges and the media have resolved the inherent difficulty in marketing to a community when an institution's identity is at best diverse, and, more often, difficult to define.

Johnson (1979) provided early insight into the "marketing" role that the media plays as community colleges attempt to advance and disseminate their programs and advertise the purpose and identity of each college to the community at large. Johnson defined marketing as a combination of promotional activities and programs designed for certain demographic groups.

Even in the late 1970s, Johnson was clear when he stated that college leaders must understand marketing and emphasize its importance to all college staff members. Cohen and Brawer (1996) note that by 1988, a "sizable percentage" of community colleges throughout the nation had established marketing units within their colleges; this was somewhat reduced in the late 1980s because of budget reductions. It can be assumed that for the majority of these campuses "marketing" included interactions with local media outlets, including community newspapers and radio stations.

College Identity Promoted by Media

The small amount of published research documenting college-media relationships has focused primarily on how colleges should work with media representatives to ensure timely and accurate press coverage that benefits the college and its programs. Again, most community college scholars and journalists emphasize the importance of ensuring that a college have a clear definition of its mission, goals, and image, in a manner that can be easily communicated to the media and thus to the public.

Hudson (1974) addressed the Florida Association of Community Colleges Commission on Public Relations in a speech entitled, "PR: What the Media Expect from You." The purpose of Mr. Hudson's speech was to teach college public relations personnel how journalists and editors make decisions that determine newspaper content and to present the most effective ways of establishing working relationships with editors of local newspapers. His main goal was to address the question, "where does your organization and its news releases fit into [the newspaper]?" (1974, p. 3).

While the main purpose of Hudson's presentation was to inform public relations officers about how to ensure the most accurate coverage of their college's events and programs, Hudson successfully revealed the difficulties that media personnel throughout the county must resolve as they work with educational leaders. Most important, Hudson stated that newspapers "do not want to do business with an organization which operates its program in a muddled way" (1974, p. 3), lending more credence to the media's concern about how to best represent a college's programs and services in a way that accurately reflects its institutional identity.

Understanding the importance of defining a college's identity as a means of marketing programs and services to potential students, more recent research has focused closely on relations with media to promulgate and improve campus image. The *Community, Technical and Junior College Journal* published a series of essays that addressed this critical area of concern (Gehrung, Johnson, Petrizzo, and Stubler, 1986). In one essay it is stated that "success stories left unsaid are [of] no credit to the colleges without the media also there to tell them . . . [that] therein lies a public image at risk, one for which the colleges are in sore need of improvement" (p. 32). In these essays, the authors draw on their experience with community college public relations activities to advise community college colleagues in establishing relationships with the media. Gehrung, for example, notes that the amount of coverage of events and programs on college campuses is directly proportional to education's place in the public's list of priorities. "Society has education well down its list of concerns, . . . [and] media coverage reflects these concerns" (p. 33). He notes the importance of providing the media with tangible stories and events that can be reported. He states that perceptions of a community college "are not the sort a journalist can, as they say, point a camera at . . . [and that] a community college providing a damned good education to a lot of people who otherwise would not have it available is not front-page material" (p. 33).

Johnson, in the same series of essays, reiterates this point, stating that success stories that occur on a community college campus usually never make headlines for a variety of reasons, including a lack of college initiative in getting news to the media, poor writing skills, articles submitted with little or no news value, or a lack of credibility on the part of the college. Johnson believes not only that strong ties to media representatives are critical to the success of any community college, but also that the public's support of higher education is in part determined by its understanding of higher education. She notes that "it is paramount that community college news providers help reporters understand the philosophy, programs and services of two-year colleges" in order for a two-year college to be reflected in an accurate and positive manner. She states that "since the avenue for building recognition and public acceptance is . . . dependent on the news media, the quality of an institution's image . . . is largely due to its daily working relationships with reporters" (Gehrung, Johnson, Petrizzo, and Stubler, 1986, p. 34).

Petrizzo and Stubler acknowledged, even in 1986, that the advanced methods and options of mass communications make it imperative that community colleges use creativity and careful planning to establish a strong public relations system that provides them with positive, timely, and thorough media coverage. In the third essay of this series, Petrizzo and Stubler provide more practical suggestions and ideas to be used by public relations officers and CEOs of community colleges to advance and market the college's programs and services to the community, and to make the college's stories and press releases receive as much attention as possible from the media, in the context of competition for newspaper space. Current issues concerning the best way to establish strong working relationships between education and media representatives are explored further in Chapter Two.

The 1990s and Beyond: The Media's Role in Advancing College Identity

Probably the largest influence of how community colleges and the media will forge current and future working relationships to promote colleges and their programs will be the societal issues and priorities that surround community colleges and their constituents. Cohen and Brawer (1996) accurately noted that "public opinion, always mercurial, influences the colleges. Periodic disgruntlement with taxation and the rise of other priorities such as prisons and the criminal justice system sometimes translate into lower support for education" (p. 419). Community colleges will have few options but to plan accordingly to ensure public awareness of their beneficial role in society.

In addition, shifts in student enrollment determine which program areas are in greatest demand, and funding also helps determine the degree to which colleges incorporate media coverage and media alliances to promote their institutional identity. Cohen and Brawer (1996) state that two-year colleges will be expected to increase students' access to career studies and continuing education programs, and that community college attendance will be affected by the differences in high school graduation rates according to students' ethnic identity. While community colleges will continue to operate as long as there is a demand for higher education, their curricular focus will change with the times.

Perhaps of most significance will be the community college's increasing social role within the community. Because, as Cohen and Brawer (1996) note, community colleges open their doors to all citizens "to a much greater extent than any other postsecondary structure," they often find themselves in increasingly visible roles for promoting positive social change. As the need for career training, developmental education, English as a second language, and college transfer programs increases, community colleges' role in meeting the educational needs of a highly diverse population will increase accordingly. To this end, community colleges will be challenged to ensure that their institutional mission and identity correlate with the structure and function of their institution and that they are able to communicate their mission and identity to the media, as well as work closely with journalists and media representatives to ensure that current and prospective students are aware of the educational opportunities available to them.

References

Cohen, A. M., and Brawer, F. B. *The American Community College*. (3rd ed.) San Francisco: Jossey-Bass, 1996.

Gehrung, F., Johnson, J., Petrizzo, D. R., and Stubler, M. "How Can Community Colleges Work with the Media to Improve their Public Image?" *Community, Technical and Junior College Journal*, 1986, 57(1), 32–35.

Gleazer, E. "Foreword." In A. A. Witt, J. L. Wattenbarger, J. E. Gollattscheck, and J. Suppiger, *America's Community Colleges: The First Century*. Washington, D.C.: American Association of Community Colleges, 1994.

Hudson, R. L. "P.R.: What the Media Expect from You." Speech delivered at the Twenty-Fifth Anniversary Convention of the Florida Association of Community Colleges, Commission on Public Relations, Tampa, Fla., Oct. 1974. (ED 099 046)

Johnson, D. L. "Managing Nonprofit Marketing." In R. E. Lahti (ed.), *Managing in a New Era*. New Directions for Community Colleges, no. 28. San Francisco: Jossey-Bass, 1979.

La Paglia, N. *Storytellers: The Image of the Two-Year College in American Fiction and in Women's Journals.* De Kalb: LEPS Press, Northern Illinois University, 1994.

Sicking, T., and Harris, B. W. "A Study of Community College Image by a Survey of the Media." Unpublished dissertation, Nova University, 1976. (ED 130 690)

JANEL HENRIKSEN HASTINGS is the assistant dean of research and planning at Harry S Truman College, one of the City Colleges of Chicago.

2

This chapter discusses the advantages of good personal relationships between the media and community college public relations offices and how to build and maintain them.

The Importance of Being Honest: Building Relationships Between Media and College Personnel

Clifton Truman Daniel

Jonathan Noffke is the envy of his peers in the nonprofit community in Wilmington, North Carolina. The institution of which he is the director, the Bellamy Mansion Museum, gets the lion's share of exposure from the city's daily newspapers, the *Wilmington Morning Star* and the *Sunday Star-News.*

Noffke will say that it is because the mansion is a visible, established historic site and he will joke that he is photogenic and has no skeletons in his closet—at least none that do not already belong in an antebellum Southern mansion. The disgruntled among his peers might snidely point out that the newspaper's publisher sits on the board of the museum—if they knew about it. Jonathan has never had to, nor would he, trot it out. The secret to his success is simply that he is a nice guy.

These days, with people flexing their ability to reach out and touch someone—*anyone*—by almost any means imaginable, the personal touch has never been more important, especially when it comes to public relations and the media. Community college communications officers—indeed, public relations officials of all stripes—cannot afford to simply shovel their message onto the heap. It will get lost, actually ignored, without a friendly hand to reach in and pluck it out.

"There's a blizzard of impersonal communications—faxes, e-mails, e-mailed press releases—that assails every reporter," said Chicago journalism and writing teacher Hank De Zutter. "They don't know what to do with this blizzard, and sometimes they get hostile to it."

All individuals quoted in this chapter were interviewed in December 1999.

NEW DIRECTIONS FOR COMMUNITY COLLEGES, no. 110, Summer 2000   © Jossey-Bass, a Wiley company

13

Don Elkins, a reporter and news anchor with CLTV and WGN Radio in Chicago, has little time to bushwhack through the jungle of paper and electronic messages that seem to spring up on his desk each morning.

"It is really tough for me sometimes, because I am extremely busy," he said. "In a big city like Chicago, with a couple of major newspapers and a couple of major TV stations, there are certain areas in the city that are constantly being observed and constantly have priority—City Hall, the national scene, Congress. Everything else—and there is lots of everything else, tons and tons of material—comes into one spot and is sifted through."

At the *Star-News* we called it "spamming," to borrow a well-known term from the Internet (named after the famous canned meat product). A local public relations flack would fire off half a dozen copies of the same press release to half a dozen different people at the paper, reasoning that he had at least a one-in-six chance of hitting the right person. It drove us crazy because it told us the writer had not bothered to call and find out who the right person actually was. Sometimes someone took the time to call and tell him. More often, all six copies went into the trash.

The releases to which Elkins and other reporters pay attention are those that come directly to the right person and are, more often than not, from someone that person knows and trusts. "For me, at least," Elkins said, "that makes me look at the stories I hear about with more interest."

That personal relationship can give you an edge in the daily understandable competition for news space. If a reporter is juggling three stories and one of them is a story provided by a contact in the community known to the media person, the reporter *may* be more inclined to choose the story of the person he or she knows best. It will serve the reporter's viewers or readers well, and will help the reporter maintain a valuable contact that will help him or her serve those same viewers and readers in the future.

The Approach

There are as many ways of building working relationships with reporters as there are of building more casual friendships. You can meet them at parties or at professional seminars, have a mutual acquaintance introduce you, or, as Northwestern University journalism professor Richard Roth says, "you ring up your expense account and you start taking people out to lunch."

Others use a less direct approach to building relationships. Arthur Krock, Washington bureau chief and columnist for the *New York Times* in the 1940s and 1950s, used to keep an open table at the Metropolitan Club for any senators, members of Congress, cabinet members, or high-ranking military personnel who wanted to join him for lunch. In this way, Krock casually gleaned stories for the paper and for his column.

Before taking up the lectern as an associate dean at Northwestern's Medill School of Journalism, Richard Roth worked as a reporter and editor at newspapers in Buffalo, New York, and Terre Haute, Indiana. As such, he was not shy about socializing to build trust with his sources. It was a time-honored way of doing newspaper business. "When I was a reporter, I took people out for drinks and lunch and stuff as often as I could and the newspaper said that was fine," he said. The same is true for the public relations officers dealing with reporters, he added. "Get out of the office and go find these people."

"Often," Hank De Zutter said, "it pays to go bearing a gift. You bring them a story; you pay attention to what they want, and you bring it to them. When you give something to someone, their sense of fairness would make them want to keep up their end of the bargain."

Take the time to learn a reporter's professional interests, and what beat he covers, De Zutter said. Read his stories or watch his broadcasts and get an idea of how he writes or what angle he takes on television reports. And in making the first call to pitch a story, do not gild the lily.

"Leave your name and number, be polite, and in one sentence, give me a quick idea," Elkins said. "Don't get on the phone and speak for five minutes. I will pull the phone away from my ear and wave it in front of me until it is all over. That does not mean I have less respect for you or that I am less interested in the story." With the glut of ideas coming his way, he just does not have time.

Sometimes the chance to build a good media relationship drops into your lap. Oakton Community College in the Chicago suburbs has a very good relationship with its local newspaper, the *Pioneer Press,* but it has not had much luck attracting the attention of the larger *Daily Herald.* Then one day another community college in the area became the focus of a news story on new funding proposals. *Herald* reporters called Evelyn P. Burdick, Oakton's executive director of institutional relations, to ask if they could come to the campus, do interviews, and make comparisons between Oakton and the other college.

Not long after that, Roosevelt University announced that it was thinking of expanding into Oakton's territory, and the *Herald* reporters came back, asking for reaction to the expansion from Oakton administrators, faculty members, and students.

"And I used that as an opportunity then to promote new programs we have at the college and talk about how colleges are competing for students," Burdick said. "I try to use every opportunity I have with reporters to educate them in some way about the college. Sometimes the information is printed and sometimes it's not. But now that there are patterns established, I will routinely get calls from the *Herald* asking for stories or opinions from Oakton on national or educational issues."

Being Professional

Once you have a reporter interested in your idea, do not just drop it on her head and run.

Not long ago, when two brothers gave a university in Chicago several million dollars, the public relations office called the *Chicago Sun-Times* to make the announcement. But when reporter Adrienne Drell called back to find the brothers for an interview, no one could help her. The brothers were out of town on business, but no one knew how to reach them. Drell finally tracked them down herself by calling every hotel where they might be staying.

On the same story, she needed an interview with the chairman of the academic department that was receiving most of the money and was simply given his name and number. When she called the number, she was told that he was out of the country on a yearlong sabbatical. The public relations department, she said, "could have made my life easier."

"Anyone who realizes what a reporter needs is clearly a friend," said De Zutter, who has taught journalism and writing at two community colleges in Chicago—Harry S Truman College and Malcolm X College. He is now vice president of the Community Media Workshop, a group that runs seminars on media relations and publishes an annual guide to Chicago media. His advice to public relations officers who have sold a story idea is to follow through, know your institution, provide knowledgeable interview subjects, and help set up meetings with them. Do all you can to help the reporter.

"With television," Don Elkins said, "it is knowing that we are not going to be pestered by people when we are there, [and] knowing that we want something visual, statistics. . . ."

Be mindful of time constraints, whether you're calling or asking to see someone in person. And do not call on deadline, which is generally after 2 or 3 P.M. By midafternoon, reporters are struggling to finish the next day's story or edit film for the evening broadcast. Everything you say will go in one ear and out the other. In addition, you will annoy them. The best time to call is in the morning, when reporters are not only fresh but looking for fresh ideas as well. And whatever time of day you call or go knocking, keep it brief.

"I was a newspaper reporter and editor," Richard Roth said. "You have so many things to do that you do not have time to sit around and schmooze." Reporters at smaller papers have less time than those at large city dailies, "and they work a hell of a lot harder for less money," Roth said. "Leave after twenty minutes. Be respectful of that."

Do not pump a story up to be something it is not; you may wind up embarrassing the reporter or wasting his time—neither of which is good for your relationship. "I have been lucky with community colleges," Elkins said. "They don't oversell. Sometimes people in private public relations really oversell things, and when you show up, it is not what you expected at all."

If you just want to get a brief or an announcement into the paper, write the release as if you worked for the paper. All papers have their own style and formats. At the *Star-News,* for example, I spent an inordinate amount of time editing calendar briefs so that numbers below ten were spelled out and time came before day and day came before date. Most weeks, it took up my entire Friday. At the end of the day, all it took to send me over the edge was a press release from the Camp Lejeune Marine base listing an event as happening "06 October at 0800."

Write the release in the proper style and you are loved. You can pick up the paper's style from reading it for a few days, or just ask. You may even ask for a copy of the paper's stylebook, if it has one. Smaller papers are more likely to use a release as is. "I knew that if I could write the thing in their style and deliver it electronically, then I had a lot better chance of it being used . . . especially in the last few minutes before deadline," Roth said. If they have a four-inch hole and they need a four-inch piece of copy and yours is already set to go, he added, "you've got a good chance of getting it in."

If you do not get it in, do not give up. "Sometimes you may have some good ideas that I am not able to sail past the editorial board," Elkins said. "But I have your card and I know who you are, and that contact is as valuable to me as it is to you."

Do not assume that a story is dead if you do not see it immediately. Good ideas are "money in the bank," Elkins said. "I am still interested in that story. There are good ideas that capture my imagination. They don't go away. They are posted up on my board. I have little Baggies filled with them that are two years old."

If you cannot wait two years to see the story done, try pitching it to another reporter, but do give the first reporter the courtesy of calling him first. The immediacy may spur him to do it sooner than he planned.

"You cannot be afraid to pester," Elkins said. "Keep in touch," but do not ask colleagues or employees to do it for you, he added. "When a different person calls me each time, I treat it like a telemarketing call."

Knowing the Rules

Reporters are, by nature and by profession, a skeptical, suspicious lot. "The first lesson we teach freshmen," Roth said, "is the old saw that if your mother says she loves you, check it out."

Though reporters need personal contacts to do their jobs effectively, they draw a very clear line in the sand when it comes to how close they will let you get and who picks up the tab.

"It is probably one of the greatest debates in the business: getting too close to your source," Roth said. "There are journalists I know who simply have no relationships outside of work. They don't go to parties, they don't have parties, they don't do anything like that. And others are quite the opposite."

No industry-wide standard of professional ethics exists when it comes to how much free food or how many baseball caps a reporter may accept. It varies from paper to paper and from reporter to reporter. "*Tribune* reporters will not even take a note pad or a mouse pad," Oakton's Burdick joked.

Not long ago, Roth invited *New York Times* press correspondent Felicity Barringer to speak to his students. She accepted, but although Roth had no ulterior motive and did not want a story on the Medill journalism program, she would not let Northwestern pick up the tab for her flight or hotel. She even asked, jokingly, about the value of a Medill sweatshirt given to her as a memento. The *Times* has a $25 cap on the value of gifts its reporters may accept.

And oodles of little gifts come to reporters. The dark space beneath Barringer's desk at the *Times* is cluttered with what she calls *tchotchkes,* which is Yiddish for knickknacks and baubles. Most of it is old promotional material, like *Looney Tunes* and *Star Wars* CDs and a copy of the *X Files* game, sent by zealous public relations flacks. All of it will go to the *Times's* Christmas sale fundraiser. Occasionally, someone goes too far. One movie company sent a CD-ROM set that was clearly worth a couple of hundred dollars. "I was somewhat irritated because they should have known that was over the line," Barringer said.

Like any reporter, Drell will not go near a story where she may have a conflict of interest—for example, if she is related to someone involved or has some kind of financial interest. She hardly ever has to deal with out-and-out bribery.

"The question is, what's a gift?" she said. "If you're going to give me a Rolls-Royce, that's one thing, but what's the most you're going to do? Take me out to lunch? When I really know you, you pick it up today and I pick it up tomorrow."

Barringer recently had a cup of coffee with the information officer from the University of Pennsylvania. She had just turned him down on a story idea he had been pitching on the university, but to the officer's credit, that did not put even a dent in their relationship. And now the door is wide open for future stories.

"I trusted him because of the way he handled the disappointment," Barringer said. "He was a pro and went on to the next thing. And he didn't give me a thing but information, and information is what I traffic in. Leaving aside all the normal human exchange things, . . . in the end what matters is the quality of the information that comes to me. That is my bread and butter."

Being a True Friend

However you establish working relationships with reporters, go at it as you would any friendship—honestly and without expecting anything in return. Disingenuous public relations officials isolate themselves very quickly.

"They say, 'Look, I hooked you up with so-and-so and so now you owe me one,'" Elkins said. "It's like the Chicago give-and-take. You don't ever expect something in return. If you make someone feel like you expect something in return, it is a social *faux pas.*"

For museum director Jonathan Noffke, being media friendly means "letting people know what's going on . . . feeding the media a stream of reliable information about things that are not always self-serving . . . more of a friend-of-the-court sort of thing. It's not like, 'Oh, my God. Here he comes again.'"

You cannot be a fair-weather friend. Reporters who were kind enough to take an interest in your nursing students' perfect passing rate on the state exam will expect to talk to you when the president uses the honor society funds to buy a Jaguar XKE.

"I like to have [friends] in the nice times so [that] when the tough times come—like when someone takes the money or there is going to be a strike—I have the relationship to call someone directly," Drell said. "Even if they can't talk, they will trust me [enough] to tell me off the record and know that I will not violate that trust."

Northwestern had a brouhaha recently when it decided to close its dental school, leaving undergraduates in the lurch. Drell wanted to write a piece on the students, who were unhappy, to say the least. Alan Cubbage, vice president for university relations, might have ducked Drell's calls or refused to help her. Instead, he provided her with the names of the presidents of both the senior class and the dental students' association.

"She could have found that information out anyway. Why make her go through the hassle of making four or five phone calls?" Cubbage said. "I honestly believe that . . . it is better to be helpful to reporters, even when the story is difficult, because it is building long-term relationships. Be as helpful as you can while still being an advocate for your institution."

Drell no longer covers higher education but is assigned to legal affairs. Should Northwestern be sued some day, Cubbage said, a good relationship with the legal affairs reporter could come in handy. Drell agrees.

"Have some friends and be honest," she said. "Don't screw them. Be helpful, even when it is against your interests. You will always be remembered."

And always remember them. When a reporter writes a good article on Oakton, Burdick always calls or writes a thank-you note, whether she knows the reporter personally or not. One *Chicago Tribune* reporter did not seem impressed; however, later on, when Burdick asked if the *Tribune* would be interested in a six-piano concert given at Oakton, that same reporter dispatched a photographer to cover the event.

"Doesn't everyone want a pat on the back once in a while?" she asked.

CLIFTON TRUMAN DANIEL is the director of public relations at Harry S Truman College, one of the City Colleges of Chicago.

3

The media can help colleges enhance their public image and enrollment when a few proven rules and principles are employed by college administrators and other members of the college community.

Building Relationships with the Media: A Brief Working Guide for Community College Leaders

Neal A. Raisman

Few skills serve a college administrator better than working well with the public. The ability to communicate and shape messages is essential to effective marketing and promotion. A major component of shaping a college's image and perception of value in the public mind is the media. No other public sector can represent a college as broadly and as immediately as the media. Yet when confronted with the choice between getting a root canal and meeting with a news reporter, the average administrator heads for the dentist. But just as patients have learned that a root canal can be accomplished with little pain and great success, so too can college administrators learn to work with the media successfully and with very little discomfort. There are some basic concepts and rules that, if followed, can make an administrator into a "media star."

Relationship Responsibility and Control

The ultimate goal is to form a mutually beneficial relationship. Although some boards and administrators demand that their public relations people "control the media," this strategy cannot and should not be employed. The media perform a necessary and constitutionally protected function for society that must be supported even though they may print something upsetting about the college or about you. In fact, when a paper prints a story that is negative, even harmful, the college should protect the reporter's right to print what he or she wishes just as we would protect the academic freedom of a controversial speaker or a faculty member in a classroom. Furthermore,

NEW DIRECTIONS FOR COMMUNITY COLLEGES, no. 110, Summer 2000 © Jossey-Bass, a Wiley company if the reporter realizes that the college supports his or her role, this recognition becomes an important aspect of building a relationship. Moreover, a negative story may be appropriate in certain circumstances because the reporter is performing his or her obligation to report the news.

Second, the assumption that the media relations person should "control" the media indicates an incorrect belief that forming good working relationships with reporters is someone else's work rather than the president's. Good media relations must start with the board and the president; otherwise, the media person will have to spend too much time compensating for weak institutional relations with the media. Reporters always seek access to the people at the top of any organization unless they are doing a story meant to undermine the top. When they have to work through an intermediary such as the media relations person, sooner or later they begin to believe that they are being denied access.

The press is neither good nor bad. Your job is to point them in the most positive direction and clearly communicate any facts, details, or spin in a manner they will accept. To achieve this, a good working relationship with the media must be formed to increase the likelihood of getting your message and slant on a story heard or seen.

How the Media Work

To work with the media, it is necessary to have some idea of how the media work when covering your college. Newspapers, television, and radio get most of their news and story ideas from a few basic sources. The college may send out news releases to try to "plant" a story, or a reporter will get a "lead" from a source such as a student, a faculty member, a "leak," a politician, the police scanner or blotter, or another reporter. Alternatively, the story will be taken from another newspaper, television, or radio report.

With each different source of information comes a corresponding level of ownership of the story. The most effective way to affiliate on a story is to work with the reporter. Few interactions carry more weight than direct contact between the college and the reporter. If the college provides the lead, especially on a possibly negative story, the college and the reporter could thereby develop a mutually beneficial relationship, particularly as the story develops. This does not mean that the college will control the story, but it does provide the greatest chance of projecting the desired perspective. There are times when "full disclosure" can even blunt a potentially harmful story or improve weakening relations with the media.

For example, when I became president of one college, it had been under intensive attack from a newspaper reporter whom the college had been trying to lock out of a multimillion-dollar scandal story. The reporter was actively looking everywhere for negatives because he correctly believed he was being misled. The day I became president, a student worker was arrested for driving the college van while under the influence. It was found that he was also using the college credit card to buy tires and batteries, which he sold out of the back of the college van. After the sheriff's department called me about this matter, I asked a trustee for advice, and his suggestion was to bury the issue if I could. However, cover-up is never a good option because it can destroy a relationship that is based on trust.

I decided that the way to handle this was to call the same reporter who had been raising hell for the college and give him all the details. When I contacted him and gave him the full details, three things occurred: (1) the primary story, once disclosed, was no longer important; (2) the college's cover-ups ended, thus opening a new chapter for college-media relations; and (3) a direct line opened up between the media and the highest level of the college. At that moment a new relationship began, and the college started on a positive path toward gaining the needed media support to rebuild faith with the community.

Rules for Positive Media Relations

Rule 1: The media are neither good nor bad. Do not assume that the media are automatically against you. Treat them with respect and the caution that organizations carrying major public responsibility and power are due.

The media are not "out to get you" unless you give them reason to do so. Reporters are professionals doing a job. They have personalities, egos, needs, feelings, and varying levels of ability. They also carry a responsibility and a burden that most of them take very seriously; they therefore expect you to treat them seriously. As is the case with a college administrator, they are public servants whose role is to provide the public with the truth. We try to communicate truth, whether our students like it or not; similarly, the press attempts to report it, whether we like it or not. Most reporters expect that you will treat them with the respect that is due them as public inquirers. It is definitely in your interest to do so. The old rule from Rabbi Hillel follows here: Do not do to others what you would not have them do to you. Don't treat them well and they will surely not treat you well.

For example, a college president and his board members felt that they were always getting negative press, so they acted in a fairly hostile manner toward a new reporter assigned to their college and made it difficult for her to do her job. As a result, she began to resent them for treating her in an unprofessional manner. She went from being ambivalent about the board members and the president to actively disliking them. The board had to hire an outside consultant to "negotiate a bridge" to a new understanding with the reporter, based on respect.

The reporter's job is to get a story. It is the story that counts, and they will seek out the most interesting angle available. They will not, however, assume the worst, as too many people believe they will. Reporters do not start out looking to be negative, or, for that matter, positive. Reporters will actually be indifferent to a particular story unless one of three events occurs:

(1) they begin to perceive that they are not being treated with respect, (2) they believe that they are being misled to keep them from getting at the truth of the matter, or (3) they have been brought into an affiliate relationship with the college, which will incline them toward writing good stories from a positive perspective whenever they are given the chance.

The objective is to bring reporters into working relationships with the college through you, and to make them part of the college. When one feels an affiliation with a person or group, he or she will have a more difficult time being negative about that person or group.

Rule 2: Be truthful. Most people are not very good liars, so their evasiveness and prevarication are quickly caught. Reporters are taught to respect the truth and to ferret out anything that is less than truthful. If they sense that they are being misled, they will get upset and start to dig for buried bodies. If there is a problem at the college, they will learn of it sooner or later. Being truthful does not mean hanging all the dirty laundry out in public. However, it may be important to acknowledge that a problem exists and that the college knows it and is applying the proper washing and bleaching techniques to ensure that the problem does not get repeated. Reporters know that things do go wrong and will respect a forthright discussion on how the mistakes are being corrected. An open presentation of the "washing technique" rather than the existence of the dirty laundry can be made the center of an article. This approach was the core of Tylenol's success in saving the company after the poison scare.

Rule 3: The press "goes negative" when we force it to. Trying to cover up the problem will just point to the need to dig deeper and will hinder the reporter's ability to help the college create a positive situation from a negative one. If you give the full story, the reporter's job is made easier, and he or she will appreciate that and will try harder to work with you. It is human nature. Do not ask for problems. Clear them out as best you can within the limits of the Buckley Amendment and legal advice.

Rule 4: Reach out to the media during the good or at least the quiet times. Provide the media full access to the college and to those whom you wish the press to know. Call the reporters and invite them to the campus for a personal tour, during which you may point out possible stories of interest. Sit down with them over lunch in the cafeteria and then have a couple more people join you half way through. Introduce the reporters to faculty members who may have a story line to follow, or to students who are doing interesting things. Take the time to let the reporters get to know you. Also, see if you can set up a board media event during which board members and reporters can communicate about the college so that reporters can at least feel some affinity with the board. Finally, be sure to give the reporter access to you at your office and via your cell phone or home phone number. Reporters can and will get access to them anyhow, so you may as well reach out and help them. And they will appreciate it, since most people make them work to get this kind of access.

Rule 5: Every discussion with the media is an interview. Know how to interview. One of the most important parts of media star training is learning one-on-one interview techniques. Keep in mind that every time you talk with the media it takes the form of an interview. You may not be able to control the conversation completely, but with appropriate planning you may be able to guide the discussion.

Using the Interview

Interview Principle 1: A good candid interview must be prepared for and scripted. Just as some of Groucho Marx's best "ad-libs" on his television show were written and practiced in advance, "candid remarks" must be planned, scripted, and rehearsed. Begin by creating a list with two columns: one column for the topics you wish to discuss and one column for those that the reporter may want to cover. Leave enough space next to each item to jot down more information. Simply brainstorm to create these lists, and do not hold back from putting down either really positive "puff pieces" that seem self-serving for the college or the possibly damaging issues or questions a reporter could ask. Start by prioritizing both columns on the list. Place your most positive stories at the top of your column and the most possibly damaging ones at the top of the reporter's column.

Then prepare a brief statement or "sound bite" for every one of your positive statements. The bite should follow the normal reporting story line of *who, what, when, where, why, how much,* or *how it will be done,* whenever possible. The bite should also be "front-loaded" with information to lead the reporter into the statement. Be sure to frame the bite with enough substance to attract the reporter to your story. Do not just put the story out there as an understatement. For example, a college president announced to a reporter simply that "the college will not be raising tuition next year." The reporter did not catch any enthusiasm or a strong enough angle to get excited. The story was a mere mention when it could have been a very positive lead.

The president should have at least begun the statement with a sympathetic *who*—students and families, then *what*—"will not have to worry about an increase in tuition at the college next year," to follow with *why*—"because we have costs under control."

An even stronger frame would have been to open with a more dramatic statement to grab the reporter. For example: "Increasing tuition at some colleges has placed an undue burden on students and their families, so this college will not raise tuition next year. We are able to do that because we have worked diligently to get our costs under control so families will not have to be hurt." These statements frame the story for the reporter and direct him or her to follow up on (1) the concern that the college has for its students, (2) what other colleges are doing (3) whether tuition was raised before and how much will it be next year, and, most important, (4) what the college did to control costs. Therefore, prepare responses to these issues as well.

Interview Principle 2: Have responses ready for any possible negatives that may arise. The goal here is to head off any questions that may be harmful. Keep responses brief and, whenever possible, place a positive light on a contrary question or probe. For instance, when an administrator was asked about a rumor of a sexual harassment problem with a faculty member, she replied, "I heard about that and was horrified." This answer made it appear to the reporter, first, that there was a basis for the rumor (when there was not); second, that she was aware of the details; and third, that there was a good story here. When pushed by the reporter about details, she said, "Well, I can't provide any at this time." This added to the reporter's interest, since now it seemed that she might have details but was not being forthcoming. The final result was a story that said that there was a problem at the college and that the administrator was refusing to be honest with the paper.

The answer should have been something like "We do not respond to rumors. But let me tell you about the sexual harassment policy, procedures, and training we have here at the college." This would have indicated that there would be no statement on a rumor, while giving the reporter another way to phrase the story—or drop it.

Interview Principle 3: Not every question calls for an answer. In the situation just described, the statement "I'm sorry, but we do not respond to rumors" could have sufficed. The reporter would probe again and possibly again and the answer could remain "We do not respond to rumors." The reporter may come at it from another angle, such as "How many sexual harassment cases have there been in the past year?" If you do not know, simply say you do not know. Keep in mind, though, that when anyone speaks in one's capacity as a member of the college community, that person speaks for everyone. With that in mind, try to use "we" or "the college" when speaking. Use "I" sparingly and when you want to try to distance remarks from the college.

Interview Principle 4: Do not volunteer anything that could be turned into a negative. If you wish to bring forward information that could be seen as less than positive, be certain that this has been well planned and for a specific purpose, as in the example of the student arrested for drunk driving. If you are unsure, simply state "I cannot speculate" or "It would be wrong to guess." If at all possible, find a replacement for "I cannot comment." This phrase will only bring additional probing, since it is seen as an implied statement of wrongdoing. Another fully acceptable response is "The issue is under review, and I will get back to you when it is resolved." Have a possible date for conclusion and response, since the reporter will almost always want to know when.

Interview Principle 5: If possible, try to "interview the interviewer." Done correctly, interviewing the interviewer can be a potent relationship builder. The basic concept here is that you get the reporter talking so that the initial questions and comments come from you, not from the reporter. People love talking about themselves, particularly if they are engaged in an activity that most people either do not understand or dislike. The media have both counts against them, so reporters are often eager to explain themselves and to defend their job. A good opening can be an empathetic statement such as a reference to a letter to the editor from the morning paper that complained about some aspect of the paper's coverage. "It seems you folks can't even print a bake sale without someone complaining that you forgot to mention someone's apple pie" was one I used when someone wrote in to complain about a humorous column about judging a baking contest.

Interview Principle 6: Do not allow yourself to be interrupted when making a statement. Too many college administrators try to be too polite during an interview, and they allow a reporter to interrupt an answer with another question. This is a method calculated to catch you off guard so that you make a mistake in your response. Complete your statements.

Interview Principle 7: An interview is a performance—so practice. Prior to meeting with a member of the media, practice your prepared statements with a small audience. Have the audience members play the role of the reporters. They are to probe your statements, ask questions, and critique your responses. They should also watch you—your facial expressions and your body language. These are clues that we focus on when conducting a media star training session. Listen to their comments or criticisms because they will often be valuable. Although your written responses may be wonderful, they must sound right. If they do not, they are not right no matter how factual or well constructed they may be. An interview is an audio and visual performance. It is also a good idea to audio- and videotape the practice session. Watching it will help, but listening to the statements is even more informative. If some statement from you does not sound right or real, change it to sound more sincere. You must get comfortable with yourself if the reporter is to do the same.

If the foregoing principles are followed, better media relations will ensue. Reporters respect someone who can make their job easier, who can give them leads and stories, and who interviews well. Positive working relationships are based on mutual respect and association. Good media skills will help form that partnership with reporters. In turn, the college will get better, or at least fairer, press coverage.

Neal A. Raisman is president of Academic MAPS, a full-service collegiate consulting firm.

4

This chapter deals with the relationship between community colleges and the media: what journalists expect from community colleges and how community colleges can get more of what they need from journalists.

Community Colleges and the Media: Getting Effective Coverage for Your Institution

Tim Thornton

Reporters who cover higher education want a lot of things from the people in collegiate news services, information offices, and external communication bureaus. But most of those wants can be boiled down to one thing: a good relationship.

Don Patterson, who covered higher education for the *News and Record* in Greensboro, North Carolina, for seven years, got a chance to address a group of people who represent colleges to the press and the public. He delivered a simple message: "The thing I told them [that] was most important," he said, "was to have a personal relationship with the reporter" (interview, Nov. 1999).

Like any relationship, the relationship between a reporter and a communications officer requires understanding as well as respect and trust. Respect and trust are things that must be developed between people, but understanding is something you can find on your own.

Patterson said he tries to build understanding through what he calls good old boy journalism. He tells sources, "I'm not the smartest guy in the world, so you're going to have to help me out."

"One of the best things I did when I got the job was to go on a tour of the colleges here," Patterson said. "At some places it was like I was a celebrity. They brought people in to see me." That gave Patterson and people at the colleges he covered a chance to put faces with names—a chance to get some sense of whom they were dealing with.

Beth McMurtrie is a writer with the *Chronicle of Higher Education.* Her reporting style has a harder edge than Patterson's, but she, too, encourages public relations professionals to go out of their way to meet reporters and to set up meetings with senior officials and other people who will be dealing with the press.

Openness Versus Secrecy

Generally, secrecy is bad and openness is good. McMurtrie said she wants three things from a public information office: access to people, timely responses, and complete information. "If you're denied any of that, it sends up red flags," she said. She adds that reporters "tend to be skeptical people" (interview, Nov. 1999). When a college seems reluctant to share information, reporters tend to assume that the institution has something to hide.

Institutional reticence makes Patterson uncomfortable, too. "That sense of drawing in—you don't ever look good," he said.

A university I occasionally deal with was recently involved in two stories that were not likely to make the school look particularly good. The stories were related, though they broke weeks apart.

In the first story the program manager and news director of the public radio station on campus resigned because of the station's coverage of a controversial campus story. They had been told to limit their reporting to reciting the university's press release. The university official responsible for that decision eventually apologized and suggested that responsibility for the station be transferred to another department. It was. Nevertheless, the station's news executives resigned.

The station manager would not return reporters' calls; she simply told the school's news service when the calls came in. The news service didn't call back either. The only person authorized to speak for the university on the subject was an assistant provost. He was at a conference halfway across the country. Eventually, the assistant provost returned the reporters' calls, but he'd been given charge of the station just three days before, as he kept saying, so he really didn't have a lot of insight into the issue.

The upshot was that the university looked secretive, censorious, and disorganized, while the people who had resigned—who had less than flattering things to say about the university—got a thorough airing of their opinions in the media.

A few weeks later, the Protestant denomination that founded that university announced its intention to sever all ties to the school. The first official line from the university was that there would be no official line from the university concerning this milestone in the university's life. The university news service seemed to have difficulty contacting any of the school's professors whose disciplines made them experts on the church, the school, and the relationship between the two institutions. One professor who had given an extensive interview about the history that tied the school and the church together called a reporter back to ask that nothing he said be published. The president had issued an edict forbidding everyone at the university to speak to the press about the issue.

Eventually, the edict was reversed and the president issued a statement on the church's decision, but for most of a day, the school again looked as though it was afraid of public scrutiny and therefore built mistrust with the press.

Sometimes secrecy isn't sinister, it's just irritating. A community college I cover let it be known that there would be two major announcements on campus on a certain Friday—at 6 P.M. and at 7 P.M. But no one at the school would say any more about it. I was sitting in a budget meeting listening to a discussion of what would go where in the next day's newspaper. When the editor of the paper—my boss's boss's boss's boss—asked me about the community college story, I couldn't tell him a thing. That was personally embarrassing, which certainly didn't have a positive effect on my relationship with the community college. But that wasn't the worst thing about the experience from the community college's point of view—at least in the short term. The worst thing was that the decision makers at the paper didn't have the information they needed to decide what kind of play the story should get or how much attention should be paid. As a consequence, the largest monetary gift in the history of the school, as well as the announcement of a new school of entertainment named after a famous country music performer, appeared deep inside the newspaper without even a photograph to draw attention to it.

A public relations officer from another college called to tell me that there would be an announcement at his school at the end of the week—but he couldn't tell me anything about it unless I promised not to write anything about it ahead of time.

The standard procedure at my newspaper is not to enter into any such deals. Occasionally, we'll agree to hold a story until the day of the announcement. But if we wait until the next day to publish the announcement, the newspaper will be behind television, radio, and our own Web site, with the news. If that's going to happen anyway, there's no practical advantage to knowing anything ahead of time.

No one I know of would agree to an embargo before knowing something about what's being embargoed.

In this case the public relations officer went over my head. He called my boss, who weaseled out of him what the big announcement would be. It was the beginning of a fundraising campaign. Neither I nor my boss had a problem with waiting to publish that story. But the decision had to be ours. That's just the way newspaper people are—they feel that they should be able to decide what goes into their newspapers.

Preparing for Difficult Stories

Patterson offered this advice to public relations professionals confronted with an unflattering story: "Suck it up. Spin where you can, but it's going to be a story."

When a student died on a public university campus that McMurtrie was covering before she joined the *Chronicle,* the school refused to release any information about the event, refused to release the student's name, refused to cooperate with the newspaper at all. When McMurtrie went on campus to talk to students, the school's public relations officer and her boss responded by visiting McMurtrie's editor.

The university representatives compared McMurtrie to a vulture and said that the only way to rebuild relations between the paper and the school was for McMurtrie to call the public information office every time she was coming on campus. When McMurtrie and her boss refused, the university people stormed out.

That didn't do a lot to build a positive relationship.

If you build a relationship during quiet, routine times, things will run more smoothly during times of stress. In McMurtrie's example, the relationship between the public information officer and the reporter was pretty weak in normal times, so it cracked quicker under stress and left not much to build on when that particular brouhaha was over.

Patterson said that Duke University had the best public information office he had ever dealt with. "They took time to educate me," he said. "What I admired most about Duke [was that] they admitted they weren't perfect. They didn't try to hide problems. They didn't try to bob and weave and shuck and jive. They just said, 'We have a problem and here's what we're going to do to address it.'"

Which leads to another important piece of advice from Patterson: "Tell the truth."

"I always wanted people to tell me the truth," he said. "Don't be afraid to tell the truth."

Not everyone is courageous enough to do that. When he started covering colleges and universities, Patterson said, "I didn't know much about academic freedom, but I thought it would mean everybody would say what they know. Boy was I dumb."

Knowing Your Campus

After truth, perhaps the most important thing a public information officer can trade in is accuracy.

I was assigned to cover a discussion of evolution and creationism on a college campus I don't usually cover—a campus that was far enough away from my newsroom that I couldn't drive back from the event to write my story. I would have to file electronically to make my deadline. So I called ahead to make sure there was somewhere I could file from. Someone in the campus news office told me there were plug-ins all over the building I could use to modem my story to my newspaper. It turned out that the plug-ins were for the on-campus Ethernet, and so I couldn't use them. I couldn't use the only public phone jack in the building, either, because I didn't have the campus code number necessary for long-distance calls.

A student working on a laptop offered to e-mail the story through his account. The e-mails got to my office about four hours later. I had to dictate the story over a pay phone. That's a small thing, but it shows that the people charged with distributing information don't know as much about their campus as they should.

You should know a lot about your campus—the history, the people, the programs. A reporter won't take you seriously, McMurtrie said, if she feels that she knows the institution better than you do.

Knowing All the Details

It's a good idea to know the stories you're pitching, too.

McMurtie said, "A bad PR person will call me up and say, 'I've got this new program going and I think you should write a story about it'"—and then he or she will not be able to answer any questions about it.

If it's not important or interesting enough for you to find out about it, why should the reporter care? And then why should readers, viewers, or listeners care?

"The best PR people are almost like journalists themselves," McMurtrie said. They put the story they're pitching into some kind of context. They can tell a reporter why someone who's not part of the college family would want to hear the story they're pitching.

"Try to put yourself in the mind of the readers," McMurtrie advised. Ask yourself, "Would you read this story if you didn't work on campus?"

McMurtrie also advises: "Don't keep pitching puffy stories." That doesn't mean you shouldn't pitch positive stories or feel-good stories. It means that there has to be some substance to what you pitch, enough news or human interest value to build a story around.

An award-winning feature writer once cautioned against running full steam into a story idea before you've thought it through. She once heard about a fat farm for dogs and thought it would be a wonderful feature story. It wasn't. "There's a fat farm for dogs," she said. "That's kind of funny but that's not a story. It's a sentence." There's not much to add to that—at least not much that's interesting, informative, or entertaining.

Opening the Lines of Communication

Realize that not every idea you pitch will become a story, but don't let that stop you from making pitches. Keep in touch with the people who cover your school, even when you don't have a story to pitch, and even when you have a complaint.

"A lot of times you hear weeks later that someone was unhappy," McMurtrie said. Which doesn't do much good.

If there is a factual error in a story, you need to contact the reporter as soon as possible; every responsible news outlet is eager to correct any errors it makes. Of course, every complaint you have won't be about facts; some will be about tone or tenor or placement. Don't hesitate to take those complaints to reporters as well. Many of those problems will be beyond a reporter's reach, but that dialogue is vital to building a relationship. Letting a complaint fester accomplishes nothing good.

And one more thing from McMurtrie: "Don't demand that all media calls go through you." Do all you can to make administrators and faculty members feel comfortable with and therefore accessible to the media. They can help you build a relationship between your school and the media. Encourage reporters to use your faculty members as sources in stories that have nothing to do with your institution. This helps the reporter, gives you a chance to chat for a minute, and, if the reporter uses the faculty member in his story, helps build a positive image for your school.

Trusting Reporters and Teaching Them to Trust You

"In some ways," McMurtrie said, "I think you have to trust the reporter." Most reporters are probably worthy of your trust. Those who aren't will reveal that pretty quickly. But you have to know that your agenda and a reporter's agenda will not always be the same. You're trying to spread the good news about your institution and put the best face on any problems your institution may have. A reporter is—or at least should be—trying to paint as accurate a picture of your school as possible. Patterson calls it being "a loving critic."

That brings us back to where we began. It's important to have a relationship with people who write and broadcast stories about your school. Talk to them, help them, find out what they need and expect, and see to it that they get it on your campus. Build a relationship grounded on understanding, respect, and trust.

"I just found it the best way to get stuff into the paper," said Patterson. And isn't that the point?

TIM THORNTON is the higher education reporter for the News and Record *in Greensboro, North Carolina.*

5

How can community colleges use newspaper resources to best promote their institution? This chapter discusses the best practices.

Community College Advancement Through Relationships with the Newspaper Media

Anthony Marquez

Community colleges are important institutions to local communities. In turn, local news about community institutions is what newspapers value. The question remains: how can and should newspapers and community colleges create a relationship that is both respectful and mutually beneficial? This chapter addresses this issue from the perspective of the newspaper media.

These suggestions come from fourteen years of journalism experience, working with various institutions, including community colleges. Previously, I spent five years as managing editor of a daily newspaper, the *West County Times* in Richmond, California. This small newspaper, serving a number of cities and located near a quiet community college—Contra Costa College—in San Pablo, gave me valuable firsthand experience in how newspapers and community colleges work together.

It is clear to me that both newspapers and community colleges can do much more to improve the flow of useful information. It is crucial that colleges better understand the needs and processes of a newspaper. Community colleges should consider launching a few initiatives to create an agreeable working relationship with the press. Here are some ideas:

Become acquainted with the "beat reporter" in the college's area. One basic step for a community college is to initiate general informational sessions with the beat reporter who is assigned to cover it. The topics that should be covered include extensive background about the college as well as procedures for how the college will communicate with the newspaper. It would

NEW DIRECTIONS FOR COMMUNITY COLLEGES , no. 110, Summer 2000   © Jossey-Bass, a Wiley company also be a good idea to suggest and help set up interviews between the reporter and key contacts at the college, including senior administrators and professors. For example, Contra Costa College has a very good biotechnology department, but I did not know this until several years after I became managing editor. When a department has an outstanding reputation or excels in any way, it is always a good idea to be aggressive in telling a reporter all about it.

Become acquainted with the education editor of the newspaper. Another logical step would be to hold similar informational sessions with the editor who oversees coverage of the community college. This person is usually the direct supervisor of the beat reporter mentioned earlier. I would recommend inviting a senior editor to attend, too, if possible. These sessions should be open, honest, and earnest conversations. The college should share as much information as it can about its programs, faculty, and students. In turn, the community college can be opportunistic, taking the occasion to ask the newspaper for information about its news coverage, policies, and practices. College administrators should make sure that they walk away with a list of newspaper contact names and telephone numbers, and they should also provide such a list for the newspaper to use. The goal here is to create an open and continuous line of communication.

Take advantage of opportunities to know the paper staff. It is also a good idea to look for opportunities to get to know the newspaper and its journalists. Newspapers will sometimes hold "open house," or they will hold other community meetings in an effort to reach out to their readers. For example, at one newspaper I worked for, we held "get to know us" meetings with our readers. I recall one rather successful meeting in which we targeted nonprofit organizations. We included a panel of reporters and editors who spoke about how the news process works and how nonprofits could get their news into the newspaper by communicating more effectively with them. These sessions usually included a question-and-answer segment, allowing for more focused questions from the public. This is usually a good time for community institutions, including community colleges, to discuss and explain relevant things about the college, its key missions and goals, the composition of its student body, how the college benefits the local communities, and special programs it offers that cannot be found elsewhere. It is important that the representative of the community college make these points during this question-and-answer session because it is an excellent way to get the message out about the college while attracting the attention of local journalists.

Attend town hall meetings and forums. Another kind of public outreach that newspapers host, to which community college practitioners should send their own representatives, are what are called "town hall" meetings. At these events the target audience is, in a sense, the entire community, and not just a specific special interest group, such as a nonprofit organization. In town hall forums, a newspaper is likely to present a much broader program about its coverage and how it goes about covering the communities it serves. For example, the panel of reporters and editors will discuss coverage in all the sections of the newspaper—from local news to business to features. While the topics and the discussion will most likely be general and wide-ranging, community college representatives should take advantage of any "open comment" or question-and-answer portion of the meeting to talk about their institution, to make a "pitch" for why the college should be covered in the newspaper, and how it, too, serves the community.

Establish processes that enhance open communication. A mistake I have seen numerous times is when an institution appoints a "spokesperson" to deal directly with the press. While this, in theory, should make the process of communication better, it invariably becomes a barrier to open communication. The danger is that one person without adequate supervision can delay or try to quell news stories that he or she does not like. If the story is "positive," the spokesperson is happy to oblige by setting up necessary interviews and giving information to a reporter. If the story is "negative"— for example, a shooting on campus—the spokesperson may spend more time trying to "spin" the conversation toward something more positive. Thus, timely and important information is not shared, which leads to tension and mistrust. Because the press is not in the business of public relations, it must quickly and accurately report important news—which can sometimes be something unfavorable about a community college or other community institution—to its readers. The story will be published by a newspaper or aired on television, or, increasingly, it will appear on the Internet. It is important to remember that it is better to help reporters reach key college officials and get timely information because that can only help make the story fairer and more accurate.

One example of the pitfalls noted above comes from my days as the managing editor of the newspaper in Richmond, California. Richmond, which is the largest city in Contra Costa County, decided at one point to hire a spokesperson. As editor of the town paper, I met with the city manager and other Richmond city officials, and, of course, with the spokesperson. The subject was how this spokesperson would do his job and how it might have an impact on current relations between the city and the newspaper. All the "right things" were said at that meeting. The spokesperson would just be there to facilitate communication, and so information would flow as freely and efficiently as always, and the relationship would remain as positive. I raised concerns, from the perspective of a newspaper editor, about what might particularly happen with the communication of information on stories that could be perceived as negative. No, I was assured, the spokesperson would not be a barrier to keeping city government open or keeping the public informed about the city's business.

As expected, things started out well enough but soon turned troublesome. After two weeks it became very hard to reach key city officials in a timely manner, and if the story involved anything considered even remotely negative about the city, the spokesperson truly became a barrier. The new administrative structure that had incorporated a city spokesperson caused the relationship to suffer rather than flourish. When basic information is not shared, especially involving a public institution that runs on taxpayer funds, mistrust festers. Unfortunately, a feeling that the institution is trying to hide something is probably going to arise at the newspaper. The best policy is one of openness; it is not possible to hide bad news, so any effort to do so will only make matters worse. A community college or other institution that hires a spokesperson to deal with the press is not necessarily trying to hide something, and such an arrangement should work better than it did in Richmond.

By contrast, there are plenty of examples of good working relationships that owe their success to smart spokespersons. This issue is important to note, however, because if the spokesperson's responsibilities are not aligned within an institution's commitment to providing open and candid information to newspaper and other media representatives, the negative impact on a community college will be apparent.

Getting Started

There are other "best practices" that can help a community college put its best foot forward and result in a win-win situation for the newspaper and the community college. One recommendation is to make use of what everyone knows about newspapers, including their desire to cover "breaking" news, write about things that are unique or unusual, and report on "human-interest" subjects. With that knowledge, community colleges can review what they do on a daily basis and make suggestions for coverage when suitable occasions arise.

To determine how your college's unique attributes, stories of interest, and students may be positively covered by local newspaper resources, it is important to consider some basic questions: What makes your college unique? Which of your departments have state or national reputations for their work? Do you have any academic accomplishments by your professors and students to publicize?

Once these questions are answered, it would be a good investment for the college to put together a list of potential stories—about interesting professors or students who could be profiled, or newsworthy information about high-achieving departments at the college. Draft a simple one- or two-page press release to the newspaper with this information, and include contact information for the subjects mentioned. This is an excellent start that might result in press coverage. Once again, wide distribution of such a list is highly recommended. Send it to the reporter and editor, and even to the top editor at the newspaper. A newspaper tends to receive many press releases, but at most newspapers, good editors and reporters carefully review what they receive in the mail, especially from an institution the newspaper regularly covers. The chances of getting interest from a good list of story subjects and ideas may be higher than you might expect. It certainly cannot hurt.

A related question that comes up is whether to follow up with a telephone call, or whether to try to pitch a story idea by phone. As a newspaper professional, I would discourage this. Newspaper people are typically inundated with many calls throughout the day and face strict publication deadlines; therefore, telephone time is severely limited. It is much easier for a reporter or editor to peruse something—to see your story in writing—when time permits and when the unpredictable crush of news recedes. A press release best serves this purpose.

Another recommendation is to be vigilant about finding out about any developments related to your community college—such as a prestigious award received by a professor, a student, or an academic department or program—and ensuring immediate delivery of that information to the beat reporter and his or her editor. The sooner a newspaper gets information, the better and more thorough job the newspaper can do in its reporting. And that is good for all involved.

A "best practice" community colleges can incorporate is to routinely give newspapers information regarding upcoming college events. This has two benefits: (1) it gives newspapers an opportunity to plan future coverage—if they decide the event is newsworthy, and (2) it provides newspapers with good "community calendar"-type news that it can print. Newspapers nearly always publish consumer-oriented listings that are useful to readers, and this is something that institutions and nonprofit organizations can use to inform the public about its events.

There is another good reason to provide as much information as possible about the college to a newspaper: there might be other uses for this news at the publication. For example, there may be a weekly "community news" section that goes inside the "regular" daily newspaper. This section is usually focused primarily on community news, and it has a great need for community information of the type that a college could provide on a routine basis. Some news organizations put out separate weekly newspapers on top of the daily paper, so, again, there is a need for additional community information. A community college could get a tremendous amount of news coverage by just being aggressive in sharing information about its activities and its interesting faculty members and students.

Conclusion

The hallmark of a successful community college media outreach effort includes establishing direct lines of communication with the local press, providing background about the college, sharing contact numbers of key college officials, and ensuring prompt alerts to the press about news and upcoming events. In the end, open and honest communication still remains the best practice of all.

ANTHONY MARQUEZ *is assistant bureau chief for the Associated Press in San Francisco. Previously, he was Bay Area editor at the* San Jose Mercury News *in San Jose, California. He also worked for five years as managing editor of the* West County Times *in Richmond, California.*

6

How can community colleges use the tools of the trade within the media to their best advantage? This chapter provides examples of the best practices and offers practical suggestions for using resources available to everyone.

Working with Media Outlets to Communicate with the Public

Mark L. Wallace

In recent months, community college public relations professionals have heard two authorities on higher education—one a reporter for the *Wall Street Journal* and the other a chancellor of one of the nation's largest community college districts—reveal a fact not often discussed about community colleges: most community college students will not transfer to four-year colleges and universities. They point out that community college leaders need to recognize this truth and to reexamine their role in American higher education and in the national economy. Both speakers were applauded for speaking this truth aloud. Community college public relations professionals have an idea of who our students are, how they arrive at our doors, and where they are going. Yet this often conflicts with the institutional desire to build a positive, prestigious image based only on transfer rates.

In this conflict of image versus reality, public relations professionals must market their colleges as being all things to all people. Community colleges are in the business of selling educational products to a diverse and demanding public. They do this while attempting to maintain a sense of traditional higher education goals and trying to provide educational products to an almost completely nontraditional constituency.

Dr. Joseph Nazzaro (1999), former president of the National Council for Marketing and Public Relations, offered a list of the "top ten issues for marketing and public relations in America's community colleges." Four of his top ten are of particular interest here:

The Internet—"Maintenance of the college's homepage is becoming increasingly labor intensive. The PR Office is challenged regularly with issues, policies, content and disputes over this new turf. Expectations of administration are high in this area, but resources allocated remain low."

Media Relations—"Differs from district to district, but continues to remain a challenge as we attempt to position the college in a favorable market niche in the community while contending with cynical editors of mainstream media who are devotees of 'hard news.' This effort is becoming more difficult for most overworked and understaffed PR offices."

Marketing—"Probably represents the most significant area of concern. The major elements of this ongoing challenge are (1) finding adequate resources; (2) managing the complicated process of outsourcing graphics, design . . . with a limited staff; and (3) developing and tending to an institutional database as marketing trends demand personalized approaches."

Leadership—"Providing campus leadership without always having the clout to do so."

Given these challenges, college public relations professionals must adopt a creative approach to marketing their institution. Part of a college's marketing effort depends on free space—column inches in the daily and weekly newspapers, free airtime on radio and television, and communication with media that generates stories about the college. When crime and regional and state issues on governance and budget monopolize the headlines, a limited amount of news space is available for marketing. The job of the public relations professional, then, is to attempt to use this space to promote, protect, and preserve the college's image.

Tools of the Trade

Twenty years ago, a news release was written on an electric typewriter, photocopied, collated, stapled, and mailed to the news media, using photocopied mailing label lists. In some instances it was hand-delivered to the newspaper office. Today that same release is produced on a computer and sent by e-mail, faxed, mailed, or posted on a Web site for all to see. If anything, unmatched levels of technological sophistication between the college and the media have eaten dramatically into the time the public relations professional has to write and produce news and feature stories. As the marketing of the community college and all of its constituent parts becomes ever more complex, public relations professionals are finding it harder to keep up with the demands of promoting stories about students, faculty, new facilities and programs, alumni, and fundraising successes.

Of course, it is the challenge of the community college public relations office to maximize the use of free media outlets to its best advantage because most college budgets provide almost no funding for even basic image and special event advertising. Some tools of the trade are essentially free and are the mainstays of the public relations function. News releases, sports releases, calendar listings, and radio public service announcements capture free media space. Small financial investments in collaborations such as underwriting public television programs can also yield greatly increased coverage of college events.

Newspapers. Who reads the newspapers? Public relations professionals know that trustees, presidents, and legislators read the newspapers. In addition, most dailies have advertising and marketing departments that do research, and they can indicate who their readers are. It is also important to know who is not reading the newspapers because this could be a population for whom community colleges need to find other marketing tools.

Short, concisely written news releases targeted to reporters and editors, followed by phone calls when an issue is either timely or urgent, will generate interest and perhaps column inches. The public relations professional knows the interests of reporters and editors, and what audience the newspaper is targeting. Once a reporter's interest is secured, he or she has to sell the story idea to an editor. When all of these ingredients are combined, a story will sometimes result, but the reporter will write it, based on the original news release. Most reporters and editors use releases as a starting place to build their own stories. Small weekly newspapers will often use short news releases almost without editing, if the editors trust the quality of the work they receive from the college.

This also holds true for feature stories. Again, based on developed relationships, the reporter chooses one or several angles in a tightly written feature story to develop into a longer piece. James Carnett, community relations director at Orange Coast College, in Costa Mesa, California, is one of the most successful and honored writers in the West. Year after year, his feature stories turn into long features in the local newspapers, including the *Los Angeles Times* and the *Orange County Register.* Carnett provides reporters and editors with well-written stories that are full of angles, so that the media can further develop and take ownership of the stories.

News and feature stories can be pitched to various sections of the newspaper. At Pasadena City College, a complex story on a new method of general contracting for the new $22 million physical education and sports facilities was too lengthy and heavy with financial detail for the news section of the local daily newspaper. Working with the education reporter, the story was pitched to a business reporter and got fair coverage in the business section while the major donors to the project were being announced in the sports section, and the groundbreaking story was covered by the news section of the newspaper. Working with the beat reporter, all parts of this story came together to create for the public the image that the college had found a cost-saving way to build a major facility, develop private funding sources, and celebrate a groundbreaking.

Often overlooked for its indirect publicity about the college, one of the most successful areas for community college coverage is the sports section. Suburban dailies and weeklies will give a lot of space to community college sports, because they are interested in covering local neighborhood sports. And let's be very clear: this is men's *and* women's sports. They do this better than the big dailies and they know that this is what their sports readers want. Sports reporters run from game to game, so it is important for community college sports information directors to have as much detail available as possible before and after games for those reporters. Media guides, team rosters, and contact with coaches and players are all essential ingredients for successful coverage.

The calendar listing for college events can generate up to 30 percent of an audience. Well-planned student performance events will generally get no more than brief mention in the newspaper calendar section. Full news releases for most events are not needed unless the newspaper wants more details. But a consistent, timely flow of calendar listings will keep the college visible in the same place in the newspaper week after week, and audiences will learn to look for those listings. There are always places for longer features, reviews, and even photos to promote events, but trust the listings—and make them as complete as possible.

Larry Wilson, editor of the *Pasadena Star News,* said that daily newspapers are very aware of the community colleges in their areas. Editors are serving the same populations and are keenly aware of the population changes within their readership. As they try to tune their coverage to reach new readers, they see the community colleges responding to the same changes in the community. In one sense, according to Wilson, newspapers and colleges are trying to market to the same population—the one that is growing most rapidly.

Wilson advises that "good art" is essential in newspaper editors today. The old style of "grip and grin," posed photos is of no interest to newspapers today. Wilson said that he and his colleagues want action photos—nothing posed— photos with interest, with students and faculty members at work. A great photo opportunity will take a story a long way in the process of becoming ink.

Pasadena City College competes with the California Institute of Technology, Art Center College of Design, Fuller Theological Seminary, and Pacific Oaks College for higher education coverage in the *Pasadena Star News,* as well as with the bigger universities throughout Southern California, for regional coverage. Thus, it is essential for all relationships between the college and the media—from the president of the college and the public relations professional, to the faculty and students—to be in order, no matter what the news is.

For example, Pasadena City College celebrated its seventy-fifth anniversary during the 1999–2000 academic year. At the beginning of the year, the college held a very successful open house anniversary event. To help publicize this event, the public relations office approached both the local daily newspaper, the *Pasadena Star News,* and the largest local weekly tabloid newspaper, the *Pasadena Weekly,* for support. Both newspapers were willing to commit to publishing special sections if the college would consent to both buying an ad in those sections and to helping the newspapers find advertising support for the section. The college gave each newspaper a list of every vendor the college was doing business with in the region, and provided background material and photographs for the section writers of each publication.

The daily newspaper produced an eight-page tabloid to be inserted into the daily paper and the college bought a full-page ad, which was a partnership ad including the college foundation, the associated students, and the college's flea market. The cost of the ad was $1,200. All of the advertisers in the section included congratulatory messages as part of their ads. The newspaper designed the section and used a large number of photos from the college archives. In addition to inserting the section into the daily circulation of forty thousand, the newspaper provided an overrun for distribution on the day of the open house event and on campus during the following week, for students and the public. The weekly tabloid, with its circulation of thirty-five thousand, did essentially the same thing. Both sections became keepsakes and were picked up by the public at the event and throughout the week that followed. Additionally, advertising was bought in all of the other weekly newspapers in the college's service area to make sure every community was included in the campaign. As the anniversary continued, the daily newspaper took the initiative to cover the college's announcement of their top seventy-five alumni as a front-page story.

Without the special sections and the partnership in advertising, the college could not have paid for the coverage and publicity it has received for the anniversary. It was a matter of the public relations office creating the opportunity for these marketing ventures.

Radio and TV Broadcasters are no longer obligated to run public service announcements (PSAs). Many radio and television stations do, however, and many have a community calendar of events as well. Cindy Young, interim general manager of KPCC FM 89.3 (licensed to Pasadena City College), one of the nation's largest public radio stations and a National Public Radio affiliate, said that the Federal Communications Commission (FCC) requirements for public affairs broadcasting are a thing of the past. Still, KPCC receives hundreds of public service announcements each week but has no airtime for these announcements. Nonprofit agencies and charities depended for years on free time that has now almost completely vanished.

One way to reach public broadcasters is through program underwriting. According to Young, a number of the major performance companies and college and university venues in Los Angeles have successfully underwritten KPCC programs, offered tickets as giveaways, and boosted their box office sales. Program underwriting is far less expensive than commercial advertising, and it reaches targeted audiences. Colleges with major performance series or venues should consider ticket giveaways during public broadcasters' membership drives and program underwriting.

In the Los Angeles region, the Southern California Broadcasters Association (SCBA) was formed as a clearinghouse for nonprofit organizations to qualify for free airtime from participating member broadcasters. Nonprofits prove their status, join as members, and receive a member number that is included on all public service announcements. The SCBA also provides a list of all of the member stations, which includes station requirements for PSAs and contact people. The May 2000 list includes fifty-eight radio stations, fourteen television stations, and four cable systems. Language requirements and formats are also included on the list.

Television requirements are specific and technical, and broadcast quality is a strict requirement for television. For example, at KNBC-TV, Channel 4, in Burbank, California, only one-inch videotape is accepted. The announcements can be exactly ten, fifteen, twenty, thirty, or sixty seconds long and must be submitted on "1-inch Type C color videotape with 60 seconds of bars and tones, 10 seconds of black and 5 seconds of slate followed by 5 seconds of black, then your message. Horizontal blanking should fall between 10.7 and 11.1 microseconds. Vertical blanking should not exceed 21 lines." While you're at it, you might want to hire Leonardo Di Caprio to star in your PSA so that there is some slim hope that it will air before midnight.

KCBS-TV, Channel 2, in Los Angeles, has a different set of requirements and must receive PSA requests eight weeks before they are to air. If this is a PSA for an event, then you are looking at ten to twelve weeks' lead time. Clearly, television PSAs require long-term planning and a budget for production either on campus or by a production company, with no guarantee that they will air during peak viewing periods.

There are, however, examples of some successful regional efforts. In 1984, enrollments were dropping in most of the community college districts in the Fresno media market. Five of the college districts banded together to create a television advertising campaign. The consortium hired an advertising agency, which in turn hired a commercial producer to create one thirty-second spot. The ad agency had bought large blocks of TV time to resell to their clients, and the consortium worked with the agency and secured the single best spot on the ABC affiliate during the 1984 Summer Olympics. Just as the opening ceremony closed with the American flag being walked off of the track at Memorial Coliseum in Los Angeles, the network went to their affiliates for a local commercial. In Fresno, that was the community college ad, with the highest viewership for television that summer. In addition to the paid airtime, television stations ran the ad as a PSA. The cost of the consortium ad was $15,000, shared between the college districts. The ad ran sixty-eight times on three television stations, with twenty-seven spots appearing during prime time Olympics coverage on the ABC affiliate. That one spot was worth the cost of the entire campaign but it did not cost more than any of the prime time ads. All five colleges districts either held the line on enrollment or grew slightly while the state was still in a declining enrollment phase.

Direct Mail. In 1991, Pasadena City College stopped mailing its class schedule to all of the 160,000 residential addresses within its district. The college was over its funding cap in enrollment and over 50 percent of the students enrolled at the college were coming from outside the district (up to 60 percent today). To keep enrollment up, the college replaced the class schedule with a brochure styled as a calendar of events for the semester. The brochure is sent out as a reminder to enroll in classes, and it includes dates for admission and registration, as well as descriptions of the various student services. The calendar is mailed in advance of the fall and spring semesters and includes information on the art gallery, the music division, the theater department, lecture series, athletics, and other college special events. Enrollment has never dropped. Today only thirty thousand class schedules are produced and sold to students. As of this writing, the headcount enrollment is at twenty-nine thousand students. The calendar of events has boosted audiences for college events, and free distribution continues on campus all semester. The design includes examples of student art throughout, highlighting the talents of Pasadena City College's art and design students.

The college also mails *Kaleidoscope,* a small schedule of classes for fee-based courses offered through the Extended Learning Center. It is mailed five times a year throughout the district. This program is self-supporting and the mailer is paid for through the fees collected for the courses offered. Other college offices are invited to advertise in this publication, as space permits.

All three publications—the calendar of events, *Kaleidoscope,* and the Extended Learning Center schedule—are produced, ready for printing, by the campus staff, printed off-campus at a Web printing house, mailed through a mailing house, and then bundled for bidding purposes. The annual cost of printing these publications is $135,000.

Direct mail gives colleges the cheapest, most effective way of reaching residents in the district. This is less efficient when less than half of the student population comes from within the district and there are requirements that colleges not step into other districts when marketing. Thus, targeting mailings to identified zip codes outside the district to attract students becomes a tool that cannot be used and the success of direct mail becomes limited.

The Web Site: The Cure for the Common Cold or Three Mile Island. The college Web site is either a miracle or a disaster waiting to happen. When first developed, college Web sites were an information resource. Colleges found a new place to put everything, without much order or any real sense of what might be useful to the people surfing the Web. Technology improves speed and access, and, as student access grows, Web sites are trying to keep up without hitting a critical meltdown.

As a marketing tool, the Web site is available to anyone anywhere in the world. Image, appearance, ease of navigation, accessibility for the disabled, and quality of content are all issues in which the public relations professional needs to play a major role. At Pasadena City College, the two sections on the Web site that generate the greatest number of hits are the class schedule just before and during registration, and the open/closed class list throughout registration. The Web site does not provide on-line registration. To register by telephone, students must either jump from the on-line schedule to their telephones or have two phone lines available when registering.

The next generation of Web sites—and for many colleges the third or fourth generation—will require resources for changing technology, staffing, and staff training. Colleges are offering courses on-line. On-line admissions, registration, counseling, financial aid processing, chatrooms for college life, and even the "Webcasting" of college events—in addition to broadcasting via college radio and television stations—are all happening or are just about to happen. Contract education and telecourses, as well as distance learning courses, are becoming Web courses on demand and are all services that will change the way community colleges deliver education. The Web site can become a whole new interdisciplinary division of the college, calling on more resources from all over the college than any other division. It becomes for many people the new front door to the college and one of the college's most important marketing tools—as well as removing the need for more parking lots. However, those who do not have computer access or who are unable to use computers cannot be disregarded.

Cable Television. Community college public relations professionals need to take another look at cable television. Who is watching cable access channels? With intense growth in new television channels, there are opportunities to promote community college programming. With the cooperation of the local cable outlet, program scheduling can be arranged far enough in advance to allow for promotional opportunities.

Programming is repeated several times each week and throughout the month. Content can be almost anything the college produces, such as student art exhibits, visiting lecturers, tours of the campus, and sports events. Programming can include a magazine format program, or, in the case of one very successful effort at the Pennsylvania College of Technology in Williamsport, a cooking show called "You're the Chef," now seen on public television throughout Pennsylvania. Programs must be high-quality, and cable outlets depend on the colleges to keep to their schedules. Some cable providers have community access studios while others depend on the college to produce their own programming. Keys to successful cable television programming include being consistent, turning out high-quality programming, promoting the programming, and, possibly, finding an underwriter for the programming to help build the production budget.

Pasadena City College is in its second season of offering a magazine format show. Six thirty-minute shows are produced each year and sent out to the cable systems in the region. The college president and a professional news broadcaster are the hosts. Segments are shot around campus and in the community and are combined with in-studio interviews. Scheduling is becoming more consistent and the shows have been aired at various times throughout each month.

Some Tools Don't Always Work

A decade ago, IBM was making a major donation of industrial computer equipment to three Southern California community colleges to help start up new training programs for students linked directly to job opportunities in industry. It was decided that a news conference would be a great way to announce this multimillion-dollar partnership. The news conference was set in the World Trade Center Conference Facility in Long Beach, California, and was scheduled at 10 A.M. midweek—a prime time to catch the media.

The state community colleges chancellor, top executives from IBM's national headquarters, and top executives from the three colleges were gathered to discuss the economic impact of this major donation on the region. On that very same morning, a state legislator in Los Angeles decided to climb down into the bottom of the Los Angeles River and declare that it was a good place to put a freeway. The news crews never made it to Long Beach. The legislator and his original idea got the coverage. The IBM/community colleges news conference got some local print media attention, but not on the scale that the donation warranted. Though the news coverage was disappointing, the event, which brought top college officials and IBM executives together in one of the grandest settings in the region, helped to strengthen many working relationships between the colleges and IBM.

Conclusion

Radio, newspaper, television, and direct mail serve as solid means of advertising and marketing community college news and events to the public. Access to these media outlets through public service announcements, calendar listings, and news releases are either inexpensive or free. Sports news releases and calendar listings are important means of keeping the college visible. Coverage of college events can be enhanced by building good relationships with local media personnel. The college Web site is becoming an increasingly important means of marketing programs. Partnerships with local media outlets require a limited investment that reaps greater rewards. Even in the face of reduced funding, community college public relations officers have many options for keeping their colleges in the local spotlight.

Reference

Nazzaro, J. "Top Ten Issues for Marketing and Public Relations in America's Community Colleges." Paper presented at the annual conference of the National Council for Marketing and Public Relations, Chicago, Mar. 1999.

MARK L. WALLACE *is director of public relations at Pasadena City College. For the past twenty years he has served as director of public information at three California community college campuses.*

7

This chapter reviews literature that explores the changing role of institutional research in community colleges and its increasing involvement in marketing and institutional advancement activities in two-year colleges. A description of how marketing has been changed and informed by institutional research at a community college in Chicago is also presented.

Using Demographics and Statistics to Inform Target Audiences

Janel Henriksen Hastings

The role of the institutional researcher on the community college campus is traditionally structured to meet the data collection and reporting needs of community colleges. Cohen and Brawer (1996) note that the institutional research function within community colleges, while typically not supported within institutions, has gained recent fame, given colleges' requirements to produce and disseminate a number of mandated reports, including account-ability measures, assessment plans and programs, and strategic planning models.

In light of myriad documents and data that must be drafted, col-lected, and reported, institutional research plays an important and per-haps less recognized role in marketing and advertising. For college presidents, deans, and marketing and public relations officers, institu-tional research is critical to helping community college leaders make decisions about how best to invest their money toward marketing and institutional advancement.

This chapter will review literature that speaks to the changing role of the institutional researcher on community college campuses, as well as the use of institutional research to chart the course of marketing and public rela-tions strategies. In addition, this chapter will summarize a recent research and planning project undertaken by Truman College in Chicago that helped to identify advertising opportunities unique to the college's diverse student population and, in conjunction with media resources in Chicago, the processes the college used to restructure current marketing plans to reach the largest number of students possible.

Research and Planning in Community Colleges: Changing Emphases

The institutional researcher's role evolves according to the institution's needs and priorities. A review of current literature suggests that the function of the research and planning office changed with the burgeoning of community college campuses in the 1960s and 1970s. Cherdack (1979) stated that during the rapid expansion of community colleges during the 1960s, research offices at two-year colleges focused primarily on disseminating questionnaires, drafting grade and enrollment reports for the institution, analyzing student characteristics, and providing background information for grant proposals. Because the institutional researcher was quite a new phenomenon on community college campuses at the time, colleges typically hired researchers from the corps of teaching faculty. Few, if any, institutional researchers had received formal education and training in research methodologies.

Recent studies of the role of institutional research published in the late 1980s and early 1990s reveal that Cherdack's description of the early structure and function of institutional research remained true through the 1980s and early 1990s. Literature indicates that these same functions were prevalent within the typical responsibilities of a community college research office. For example, Frydenberg (1989) illustrates four methods of institutional research conducted at two-year colleges in the late 1980s: (1) research that is conducted to fulfill external reporting requirements and to help affect educational policy at the state and national level, (2) research that measures institutional efficiency as measured by teacher-student and full-time/part-time faculty ratios, (3) research that influences decision making for academic program development, and (4) research conducted for the purposes of institutional marketing and improved public relations.

It is Frydenberg's fourth function of institutional research—marketing and institutional advancement—that is relevant to community college administrators who will lead their colleges into the new millennium. Acknowledging that two-year colleges are challenged by the task of providing academic programs and services that are competitive with four-year institutions and for-profit organizations, community college leaders must learn how best to promote and advertise programs to as large an audience as possible within the constraints of set marketing budgets and limited institutional resources.

The notion of research conducted as part of a larger institution-wide marketing plan is certainly not a new concept within community college research. To be sure, for nearly two decades, scholars have recognized the importance of integrating institutional research into marketing strategies that inform colleges of the best ways in which to market programs and services to a diverse audience. Dann (1982) conducted a survey of forty-eight institutional members and eight district office members of the League for Innovation in the Community College to study the format of each college's marketing activities. Dann found that, while the majority of colleges were interested in marketing, only 33 percent of them at the time had established concrete marketing plans and functions within the college. Another 22 percent of the colleges had an administrator with the word "marketing" in his or her title, and 53 percent had either a marketing committee or a marketing task force. Marketing activities most frequently conducted by researchers or marketing committees included promotional programs, needs assessment studies, and the creation of marketing plans. Dann's suggestions, drafted in 1982, continue to apply to the modern American community college. She recommends that colleges identify their goals and expectations before creating a marketing plan, and that they evaluate the quality and capability of their research functions that affect their marketing strategies.

The results of Craig's survey of colleges in the Mid-Plains Technical Community College area (1991) demonstrate that college administrators' interest in using institutional research for the purposes of marketing had not waned. Craig found that 76 percent of administrators in the area felt the need to organize an institutional research function within the district. Also, 75 percent believed that the areas of research in greatest need included collecting data to influence state legislation, to support federal grants, and to augment public relations and marketing surveys.

Recognizing that there has been support in the past for integrating institutional research into institutional advancement activities, and that this support will continue into the twenty-first century, to what degree have colleges been successful at changing the process by which widely diverse student audiences are reached through marketing? The remainder of this chapter will describe a recent project completed by one of the City Colleges of Chicago that enabled research and planning activities to help shape the direction of marketing and media relations within the college.

Marketing to a Diverse Audience: Truman College's Experience

Harry S Truman College is a two-year college located on the northeast side of Chicago. As one of seven campuses within the City Colleges of Chicago District, Truman College enrolls approximately thirty-two thousand students each year. A bit of background on the structure and demographic composition of Truman College helps to establish the context in which the Research and Planning office embarked on a college-wide assessment of appropriate media resources to be incorporated into the college's marketing plan.

Of the 32,522 students enrolled at Truman College during fiscal year 1999, approximately 68 percent were enrolled in Adult Learning Skills Program areas, including English as a Second Language (ESL) and General Educational Development (GED) programs. Over 44 percent of all Truman College students are of Hispanic origin, and over 71 percent of students' self-reported income levels are at or below the standard poverty level for a family of four ($16,544, per the U.S. Census Bureau). Fall 1998 survey data indicate that Truman College students hail from 110 different countries and speak any of fifty-six different languages.

Past Marketing Strategies. Given the widely diverse student population on campus, Truman College administrators have been continuously challenged with the responsibility for creating marketing programs and services that are as diverse as the student population itself. The college offers a wide range of academic programs in credit, vocational, and developmental arenas. Between 1993 and 1998, the office of Institutional Advancement was given the responsibility for managing marketing and alumni affairs activities. In the summer of 1998, Truman College hired two new administrators to help augment institutional advancement activities: a director of public relations and an assistant dean of research and planning. Together, the three administrators began the process of rethinking how best to reach a diverse market of students, using limited available resources.

Before each class registration period, the assistant dean of institutional advancement typically designed and submitted advertisements to city-wide newspaper publications, including the *Chicago Sun-Times* and local community papers, such as *Exito, ¡Extra!* and *N'digo.* In addition, staff members at the college's Refugee and Immigrant Assistance Center invoked the assistance of employees at a local Vietnamese newspaper, a local Russian newspaper, and certain radio stations, to run advertisements for Truman College's large populations of students from both Eastern Europe and Asia.

Despite the publication of advertisements in myriad local media outlets, it was not clear whether these advertisements were reaching current and potential students. In addition, Truman College, as well as the other campuses of the City Colleges of Chicago, continued to see declining enrollments of students in all program areas. Understanding that the decline of enrollments was small yet steady, and could be attributed to any number of factors, including the improved economy in Chicago and low unemployment rates, staff and administrators at Truman agreed that the time was appropriate to rethink marketing strategies and learn how best to invest marketing dollars in order to communicate to a large student audience.

It was agreed that the best way to begin restructuring marketing activities would be to learn what students read, what they listened to on the radio, and what television stations they watched. Working with a variety of campus administrators, the Office of Research and Planning drafted an institution-wide marketing survey for the students.

Methodology. Students enrolled in credit, pre-credit vocational, and adult education classes were invited to participate in the study. Surveys were distributed during class time in approximately fifty class sections throughout the college. A total of 951 students completed the survey.

Students were asked to rate their level of satisfaction with current class registration processes in place at the college, and at the end of the survey they were asked to list the radio stations they listened to, the television stations they most frequently watched, and the newspapers they read. In addition, students were asked to indicate how they had heard about Truman College and why they chose to enroll at the college.

Results. One of the most striking results of the survey was the number of students who stated that they had heard of the college by "word of mouth." Over 74 percent of the students stated that they had learned of the college and its programs through friends or family members. It was also interesting to learn that current media resources used to advertise the college were not indicated as a typical means by which students had heard about Truman College. In fact, only 7 percent of the students stated that they learned of Truman College (or City Colleges of Chicago) through television ads, and only 2 percent stated that they learned about the college via newspaper ads. Another 11 percent stated that they had heard about Truman College through a high school or other academic counselor or advisor.

Newspapers. Although students stated that they did not learn about Truman College through newspaper advertisements, the data indicate that Truman College students are avid readers of local and city-wide newspapers. The *Chicago Tribune* and the *Chicago Sun-Times* were listed most frequently as newspapers read by students. In addition, local and ethnic community newspapers were also listed, including those in which the college has frequently placed advertisements.

Radio and television. Truman College students' choice of radio stations is as diverse as the student population itself. Survey respondents listed approximately fifty different radio and television stations that they said they listened to or watched most often. While students did not indicate radio or television as the means by which they had learned about the college, it became clear that these two media resources were viable tools for marketing and advertising.

Data Inform a New Marketing Plan. With new data now available on the media resources most used by Truman College's student body, the Office of Public Relations began implementing new advertising and marketing strategies that had not been used in the past. These strategies included the following:

• The direction of more money toward radio advertisements that would reach the Russian and Vietnamese communities in Chicago.
• The design and display of approximately forty billboards for two months throughout northeast Chicago neighborhoods, advertising Spring 1999 class registration.
• The waging, in alliance with City Colleges of Chicago, of a radio campaign to advertise programs and services throughout the district.
• The establishment of strong working relationships with local newspaper journalists—which has brought them to campus to cover stories of interest, including campus visits by dignitaries (this spring the college was visited by the U.N. Ambassador to Eritrea), art openings, and theater performances

(including the U.S. debut of Stephen Sondheim's musical *Saturday Night*).
• The establishment of a regulated process of bringing local television stations to cover stories on new academic programs on campus. For example, WGN-TV did a story on the college's new Accelerated Multimedia Training Program, which trains displaced workers to become Web and multimedia designers. Enrollment in this program reached capacity and many students agreed to be wait-listed for the program. In addition, Chicagoland Television (CLTV) came to campus to cover a new computer-based icon language literacy program, which was designed by a faculty member for nonnative English-speaking students.
• Collaboration of the faculty and staff with the Public Relations office to produce focused advertisements for a limited population of consumers. For instance, a faculty member from the communications department developed a speech communications class for working professionals. With the public relations director's assistance, they designed a flyer to advertise the new program within the college. In addition, the public relations director contacted two businesses to inform them of this unique program that may be of interest to their employees. Enrollment in this program is expected to reach capacity in spring 2000.

Conclusion

The six marketing strategies employed throughout the college are unique, in that they are standard marketing options used in new ways. The college's ability to establish working relations with representatives from the media has enabled it to achieve visibility via human interest stories as well as through traditional advertisements. The successful use of radio and billboards to attract more students indicates how student survey data have helped college administrators decide how best to redirect marketing dollars.

The effectiveness of these new strategies will be measured in two ways: (1) by determining whether any meaningful increase in enrollment has occurred throughout all program areas within the college; and (2) by conducting a second marketing survey to determine whether the college's new marketing efforts are being noticed frequently by student constituents.

At Truman College, we recognize that many questions remain to be answered in order to continue improving marketing strategies. For example, while over 70 percent of students state that they had heard about Truman College by "word of mouth," the assistant dean of research will collect more data to define what students mean by "word of mouth," to ensure that marketing efforts are reaching both the students and those who recommend the college to them. In addition, the Office of Public Relations continues to be interested in more focused marketing to smaller student populations. The director's collaboration with faculty chairs to advertise new classes and programs both within the college and in the business community is one strategy. It will be important for public relations personnel to work closely with deans and faculty members to investigate where students might come from within the city of Chicago, and to target academic programs and advertisements through media outlets that best reach a diverse student population.

In any marketing study conducted by a community college, the collaboration of both the public relations personnel and the institutional research staff will help to ensure a more effective result. It is imperative that both of these offices be involved in designing a college-wide marketing survey, to ensure that the survey will most likely include any and all questions that are relevant to both marketing and institutional research. In addition, institutional researchers must present market-specific data in a manner that is useful to public relations representatives. These data will eventually inform future marketing strategies used by the college.

References

Cherdack, A. N. "The Changing Nature of Institutional Research in the Community College." Unpublished report, 1979. (ED 186 058)

Cohen, A. M., and Brawer, F. B. *The American Community College.* (3rd ed.) San Francisco: Jossey-Bass, 1996.

Craig, F. M. "An Assessment of How to Organize Effectively the Function of Institutional Research in the Mid-Plains Technical Community College Area." Unpublished dissertation practicum, Nova University, 1991. (ED 326 283)

Dann, D. D. "The Status, Scope, and Structure of Marketing in a Selected Group of Community Colleges." Unpublished thesis abstract, University of Oregon, 1982. (ED 231 443)

Frydenberg, J. "Community College Institutional Research: What, Why, and How?" Unpublished graduate seminar paper, University of California, Los Angeles, 1989. (ED 313 061)

JANEL HENRIKSEN HASTINGS is the assistant dean of research and planning at Harry S Truman College, one of the City Colleges of Chicago.

8

This chapter outlines several ways community colleges and journalists can forge an alliance to improve their perceived roles in the community.

Making the Case for "Public Journalism"

Lucy Lee

As Arthur Cohen (1996) explains in *The American Community College,* the rise of two-year colleges in the twentieth century is attributable to multiple factors: the increasing numbers of high school graduates seeking further education, an expanding need for skilled workers, and a surge of growing communities seeking to put themselves "on the map." But perhaps the most compelling reason for the continued relevance of community colleges today is that they reflect the ideal of education in a democracy. Open access to higher education for anyone wishing to learn means that America seeks to provide educational opportunity to all, regardless of social and economic distinctions.

Connecting citizens with their leaders is also central to effective democratic decision making. The decade-old "public journalism movement" aims to enliven civic life by enhancing that connection. Mostly evident in print media, a public journalism approach to reporting on issues of public concern seeks to bridge the widening gap between the individual and government. Bridging that gap is certainly not a goal that is incompatible with the goals of community colleges; therefore, public journalism can potentially make education coverage more substantive while at the same time creating a powerful alliance between educators and reporters.

Community colleges are ideally positioned to work directly with journalists to foster and promote public dialogue about the goals, issues, and challenges facing higher education. Ultimately, both reporters and educators are in the business of responding to public needs and expectations. But understanding and fostering a public journalism approach in working with local media has another potential benefit for community colleges. Two-year institutions have a clear, central mission: working with students. But despite this anything-but-ivory-tower goal, the community college, like much of American higher education, is frequently tarred with the same brush of public skepticism that is slapped across larger and presumably more powerful social institutions. Does the general public view America's two-year educational institutions as being out of touch with public concerns?

If they do, this view is molded largely by the ways in which the media portray the entire higher education system and its complex array of problems and challenges. There is ample evidence that the public perceptions that shape American attitudes about higher education as a whole are predominantly based on what is known or assumed to be true about four-year institutions. Research on public attitudes regarding the role and function of community colleges is virtually nonexistent.

A series of reports from the American Council on Education (1994, 1995a, 1995b) highlight the willingness of the American public to believe in and support higher education, but show that support to be based more on the baccalaureate credential than on a high regard for the educational process itself. This public support may be thin because it is built on limited information. The public simply doesn't know enough about how colleges work, let alone about the breadth of educational opportunities available to students.

Where are the news stories about the costs and benefits of attending community colleges, for example? Public perceptions about college costs were overwhelmingly negative throughout the 1990s, reflected by the fact that only 12 percent of Americans described college tuition as a good value for their money (American Council on Education, 1995b). Such reports suggest that Americans are not armed with the informational tools to make distinctions between a high-cost baccalaureate education and the relative bargain of attending a community college.

This stern view of the value of college may also be a byproduct of the public debate about the waning of civic life, which intensified in the 1990s (National Commission on Civic Renewal, 1999; Pew Research Center for the People and the Press, 1998; Putnam, 1995). Some scholars and pundits accuse higher education of doing too little to foster the values of citizenship. At the same time, cynicism about public concerns is often connected with cynical news reporting (Shaw, 1996). Who is responsible for declining public trust in societal institutions and citizen indifference to fundamental civic responsibilities like voting and keeping up with political affairs? While no clear villain has emerged, it would seem that both the media and American colleges and universities have suffered a decline in public esteem. With both in need of a PR "makeover"—at least in the eyes of a jaundiced citizenry—colleges and journalists are presented with the opportunity to forge a strategic coalition. The media need to have good news to report in order to counterbalance the common view of the journalist's fundamental, misanthropic credo: "If it bleeds, it leads." Community colleges need to attract much-needed attention for themselves by capitalizing on the news media's desire to improve its own image.

This chapter outlines several ways to forge this essential alliance between community colleges and journalists covering the higher education beat. A partnership can be built by doing the following:

Developing an understanding of the public journalism movement and its potential impact on education coverage.

Exploiting the qualities that distinguish two-year institutions from their four-year counterparts. Competing with elite liberal arts colleges or research universities for media attention can be a recipe for frustration.

What Is Public Journalism?

Public journalism is a controversial movement designed to reexamine how we define the role of journalists in American society. The movement, which began taking shape in the early 1990s, asks whether reporters should function strictly as observers or as more active participants in stimulating public discussion of political and civic issues. An explicit task of the public journalist is to help media consumers become better citizens.

This new way of thinking has resulted in an alternative model for news coverage, primarily used by print media. Rather than focusing on the stories that fragment and divide us, public journalists seek out news that reflects what is healthy and positive in public life. Public journalists adopt the view that the media do not exist solely to tell us the news, but to help us care about it and act on it. Public journalism advocates see this approach as a shift of emphasis rather than as a new set of priorities.

Jay Rosen, a professor of journalism at New York University and the director of the Project on Public Life and the Press, is a central figure in the public journalism movement. In his 1996 book *Getting the Connections Right,* he chronicles the frustration of many prominent members of the media who are dismayed by reporting that is not only detached from the events being reported, but also from the readers. Rosen writes, "I once asked a former *New York Times* reporter why he left the paper near the peak of his career. He said he found it intolerable that the institutional culture of the *Times* would not permit him to care about what happens in education, his beat for a time. In upholding what they take to be their professional responsibility, journalists often reach this extreme point of isolation, where they have effectively removed themselves from the political community, whose fortunes remain their quarry but not their concern" (p. 79).

Most journalists still generally hold to the belief that they have a responsibility to provoke positive social change. But the critics of public journalism appear to fall into two camps. There are those who believe that all good journalism is, by definition, "public." The public journalism "movement," then, is simply a reflection of what has always been best journalistic practice. Another group of detractors argue that public journalism may compromise the fundamental journalistic value of objectivity. The critics come not only from the media rank and file, but also from the section of the academic community that is charged with training journalists and helping students understand the role of media in society.

Public journalism is still in its nascent, experimental phase. It requires a shift in the relationships that have traditionally existed between government, news media, and the people. The "public journalism model," in essence, requires a more actively involved public. Instead of simply interpreting issues and reporting events—serving as a conduit from government and civic leaders to media consumers—public journalism injects citizens directly into the process of public agenda setting (Denton and Thorson, 1998). To truly listen and respond to public concerns, the sacred principle of journalistic detachment must be sacrificed. Many journalists reject such a move, arguing that for journalists to align themselves too closely with public concerns is antithetical to their historic role. Despite the controversy, Rosen (1996) reports that by the mid-1990s a public journalism perspective had been openly adopted by more than 150 news organizations and had become a major topic of discussion among news professionals.

The public journalism philosophy has been discussed and debated for much of the last decade; however, there has been little empirical evidence to confirm its impact on the way reporters work. Some public journalism efforts have been rooted in an organizational restructuring of the newsroom—putting reporters in teams rather than having individual reporters cover predetermined "beats." The team approach can encourage a reporter to seek out more community-based sources and to listen carefully to citizens and how the citizens themselves define the news (Johnson, 1998). New studies are looking at the role of the public journalism model in how citizens form attitudes about issues of public concern, or whether it makes a difference in the public policies media seek to challenge or influence. *Assessing Public Journalism* (Lambeth, Meyer, and Thorson, 1998) presents a collection of articles summarizing significant research associated with the public journalism approach. For many of the journalists who contributed to this volume, considering the public journalism path in news coverage offers a much-needed antidote to "traditional" reporting, particularly of political news.

Examples of Public Journalism Projects

A number of prominent news organizations have undertaken various "civic journalism initiatives" designed to engage the public directly in a local issue or concern. Other public journalism projects have adopted a national perspective. For example, in an effort to improve upon conventional ways of covering politics, the *Observer* in Charlotte, North Carolina, designed its

1992 presidential campaign coverage to focus on issues and citizen reaction to those issues. The newspaper solicited candidate questions from readers, and a citizens advisory board helped direct news coverage of the campaign. The 1992 voter turnout in Charlotte exceeded the all-time high by nearly 30 percent, and many analysts attributed the increase to more effective and engaging news coverage in the *Observer* (Bare, 1998).

The *Herald-Dispatch* in Huntington, West Virginia, adopted a public journalism approach in addressing weaknesses in the local economy, which had been devastated by the loss of seventy thousand mining and manufacturing jobs. In the mid-1990s, the newspaper teamed up with a local television news station to sponsor a public meeting on economic development, which attracted nearly a thousand local residents. The newspaper recruited citizens to serve on a series of community task forces examining issues of workforce and industrial development, education, and training. Members of the media in this troubled area became conveners and organizers of a civic dialogue, not just impartial reporters. The effort was widely perceived as effective in opening the discussion of economic and educational concerns to a much wider audience (Rosen, 1996).

Mount St. Mary's College: Capitalizing on "Good" Community News

An awareness of the public journalism movement helped influence the media relations strategy for a two-year degree program at a college in Los Angeles. In my view, a growing "public journalism" approach in this major media market served to benefit the college as well as the news-consuming public.

From 1991 to 1996, I served as the director of media and public relations for Mount St. Mary's College (MSMC) in Los Angeles. During that period, a common slogan appeared in promotional materials for this small Catholic college (primarily a women's college). Everywhere was emblazoned the catchy phrase, "Two campuses: One mission." These four words highlighted an essential characteristic of the college that is both its greatest strength and its most daunting challenge: MSMC's two-year Associate in Arts program attracts primarily underprepared, first-generation college students. The baccalaureate program, which has an exceptional biological sciences curriculum, among other highly competitive undergraduate emphases, seeks to enroll young women at the top of their high school graduating class. In cultivating a public image for the college, how does a public relations director represent MSMC as being both kinds of institutions?

My experience was that "selling" journalists on the successes that have emerged from the two-year "community college" within MSMC was infinitely easier than touting the baccalaureate programs. Why? Largely because we took the time to tell stories about our students, and we pitched those stories to local newspapers serving the communities from which many of our students were drawn. Occasionally, this grassroots approach led, with patience, to a big "hit." In March 1993, the *Los Angeles Times* ran a piece focusing on a student who had a shaky beginning in the Associate in Arts degree program, but had gone on to earn a bachelor's degree from MSMC, and was headed to graduate school ("Making a Difference," 1993). The MSMC director of admissions was unhappy with this media exposure for the college and called me to complain that such news coverage made her job of presenting MSMC as being competitive with Southern California's elite liberal arts institutions much more difficult.

Nonetheless, it was clear during my tenure that journalists were very interested in the unique success stories emerging from MSMC's two-year program. When it was time to report on highly competitive programs or quote an academic expert, Southern California colleges and universities like University of Southern California, University of California, Los Angeles, and the Claremont Colleges were more likely to be tapped for appropriate "newsmakers." We certainly continued to pitch our president and faculty as potential sources, but MSMC also had to find a way to distinguish itself amid the glut of available institutions. In brief, during my tenure at the college we did this by using the following methods:

Pitching human-interest stories that reflected the "good news" about local students who beat the odds to succeed in college.

Providing swift access to college faculty members who were available to comment on community issues. Community colleges can connect journalists with faculty members or administrators with a minimum of bureaucratic red tape, and, of course, the colleges that can expedite the process of gaining access to a news source will become favorite resources for reporters covering local stories.

Offering the campuses as meeting places for political or community groups.

Bringing local journalists to campuses for discussions with students about current events and the role of the media in interpreting them.

Helping journalists see campus news in terms of its impact on the local economy, consumer trends, and broader civic events.

Creating stronger ties with local political leaders, as well as with businesses, employers, and civic groups, can also be a key step for a community college seeking greater visibility in the media. Journalists rely on credible sources, and they are accustomed, for better or for worse, to hearing "what's news" from government organizations or spokespeople. Ansolabehere, Behr, and Iyengar (1993) cite research on the practices of print journalists that suggests that most daily news stories begin with information from government sources. Key to raising the media profile of a community college, then, is the ability to involve local city and state officials in the college's activities and mission. These efforts at MSMC were successful largely because of our awareness of media outlets that were interested in a more community-driven approach to news coverage.

Why Should Community Colleges Care About Public Journalism?

To determine the extent to which a local print or broadcast media outlet may be employing a public journalism technique in newsgathering, community college administrators can conduct a simple content analysis of media coverage in their area. Here are some simple ways to identify the presence of a public journalism perspective:

Analyze the identified sources in news articles to see how many are citizen-based versus bureaucracy-based. Calculate the ratio.

Classify news coverage of education-related issues in two ways: those stories that primarily react to "news" generated on campus (reporting on policy announcements, statistics, appointments, and so on) and those that look at broader issues, such as challenges and concerns relating to access and equity in higher education, workforce development, remedial education, and literacy. Calculate the ratio.

Assess education stories carefully to determine whether they focus mostly on conflict, as opposed to focusing on areas of common goals and interests. Media outlets geared to a public journalism approach will be more likely to report on issues on which there is broad agreement (for example, between citizens and community college board members) rather than on areas of contention.

Clearly, community colleges will have better luck placing stories with journalists who rely more on citizen-based sources, report on broader issues, and focus at least some of the time on stories that are about common goals rather than disagreements. This simple analysis can help connect community college administrators with their best allies among local journalists—those reporters who are most likely to be interested in the people the community college serves.

Public journalism brings a value-based perspective to covering the news. If community colleges can demonstrate that the work taking place on campus is a reflection of the values of local communities, they will be able to attract the interest of the "public" journalist. Members of the media are increasingly willing to take responsibility for shaping public concerns, not merely reacting to them. In accepting this responsibility, journalists will need more opportunities to collaborate with community colleges and other local institutions directly engaged in meeting public needs and expectations.

References

American Council on Education. *First Impressions and Second Thoughts: Public Support for Higher Education.* Washington, D.C.: American Council on Education, 1994.
American Council on Education. *The Fragile Coalition: Public Support for Higher Education in the 1990s.* Washington, D.C.: American Council on Education, 1995a.

American Council on Education. *Goodwill and Growing Worry: Public Perceptions of American Higher Education.* Washington, D.C.: American Council on Education, 1995b.

Ansolabehere, S., Behr, R., and Iyengar, S. *The Media Game: American Politics in the Television Age.* Old Tappan, N.J.: Macmillan, 1993.

Cohen, A. M., and Brawer, F. B. *The American Community College.* (3rd ed.) San Francisco: Jossey-Bass, 1996.

Denton, F., and Thorson, E. "Effects of a Multimedia Public Journalism Project on Political Knowledge and Attitudes." In E. B. Lambeth, P. E. Meyer, and E. Thorson (eds.), *Assessing Public Journalism.* Columbia: University of Missouri Press, 1998.

Johnson, S. "Public Journalism and Newsroom Structure." In E. B. Lambeth, P. E. Meyer, and E. Thorson (eds.), *Assessing Public Journalism.* Columbia: University of Missouri Press, 1998.

"Making a Difference." *Los Angeles Times,* Mar. 1, 1993.

Lambeth, E. B., Meyer, P. E., and Thorson, E. (eds.). *Assessing Public Journalism.* Columbia: University of Missouri Press, 1998.

National Commission on Civic Renewal. *A Nation of Spectators: How Civic Disengagement Weakens America and What We Can Do about It.* College Park, Md.: National Commission on Civic Renewal, 1999.

Pew Research Center for the People and the Press. "Deconstructing Distrust: How Americans View Government." [http://www.people-press.org/trustrpt.htm]. Apr. 1998.

Putnam, R. "The Prosperous Community: Social Capital and Public Life." *American Prospect,* 1995, *13,* 35–42.

Rosen, J. C. *Getting the Connections Right: Public Journalism and the Troubles in the Press.* New York: Twentieth Century Fund Press, 1996.

Shaw, D. "Beyond Skepticism: Have the Media Crossed the Line into Cynicism?" (three-part series). *Los Angeles Times,* Apr. 17, 18, and 19, 1996, p. A1.

LUCY LEE *is a professor in the business communication department of the Marshall School of Business at the University of Southern California.*

9

Thanks to the Internet, more outside experts can be invited into the community college classroom than ever before. This chapter reviews innovative ways in which community colleges can train future journalists and new media professionals.

The Media as Teacher: Helping Advisers, Mentoring Young Journalists

Christine Tatum

I might as well confess that from the beginning there were times early in my reporting career when I grumbled (and not so quietly) about all those briefs and hot-weather stories I had to write. And while I am being honest, I may as well admit that I was not too crazy about all those "extra" phone calls my editor had me make or those nights he asked me to study the state's Open Meetings Act, as well as the differences between "burglary" and "robbery."

I did not understand the importance of all that then, but I sure do now—especially given my job with Tribune Media Services (TMS) in Chicago. In addition to covering higher education, I manage a journalism training program for TMS Campus, the nation's largest and oldest collegiate news service, which counts among its clients fifty-five community colleges. I am not aware of any other program like it in the country. I am essentially the editor, teacher, and "big sister" for up-and-coming young journalists. Nearly sixty students on almost as many campuses in thirty states write and produce photos, editorial cartoons, and graphics under what I hope is my careful supervision. We communicate in a never-ending wave of e-mail, faxes, and phone calls. Their work is distributed via the World Wide Web to hundreds of publications and Web sites.

The students and I walk a fine line between newsroom and classroom, and our working relationship has afforded me a unique look at what they are learning in many journalism programs and schools today. Many of their concerns are age-old, especially one in particular: how to get more "real-world" experience before graduation.

I tell them that thanks to the Web, it has never been easier.

Despite their access to technology, however, many journalism and communications students still do not understand how to use the Web to build

NEW DIRECTIONS FOR COMMUNITY COLLEGES, no. 110, Summer 2000   © Jossey-Bass, a Wiley company the portfolios they need to land their first job. For that matter, many seasoned professionals say that they, too, want to understand the Web better so that they can move up from, or out of, their current positions. While eager to pick up more technical skills, many professionals feel no need to enroll in master's programs in journalism. They are happy to take more focused (and usually cheaper) courses at community colleges—which in turn would be a smart way for colleges to improve their technology offerings and to advertise them heavily with local news organizations.

Though this chapter focuses on students wanting to enter the fields of journalism or new media, now is an incredibly exciting time to show all communications students how to use the Web to gain professional experience.

Teach the Basics Well

Because of the Internet, communication is faster and more widespread than ever. But in this business, working fast means nothing if the result is less factual.

First and foremost, instructors must continue to stress to students the importance of accuracy and fairness in journalism. Students who do not master the concepts will not survive very long on the Web, where speed rules. On the other hand, those who can consistently deliver "clean copy" will watch their stars rise fast at many Web-based organizations, which often have little time and few resources to do much editing.

Adopt a "Project-Manager" Mentality

Community colleges wanting to train future journalists should offer more courses built around multimedia projects rather than on lectures. Instructors should consider teaming with outside sources to devise classroom exercises and to come up with ways to monitor students' progress to ensure that they understand important concepts.

Devising a multimedia project to be handled by students over the course of a quarter or semester is relatively simple and requires only basic technology. Instructors at community colleges with few technological resources may want to keep projects simple by producing content only. Under such an arrangement, students would work on individual elements of a Web site. Some would write, while others would take photos or design graphics, but all would produce work that could easily be transmitted by e-mail. Instructors at colleges with greater resources might want to lead more complicated projects involving Web site design, construction, and navigation.

To find outside help, consider calling on local businesses, news organizations, and not-for-profit agencies that may want to create or update their Web site or promotional materials. Also consider the scores of Web sites out there trying to reach college students, such as www.thepavement.com, a site designed to help entry-level students make the transition from school to the workforce.

Many Web sites are happy to accept student contributions—especially those that come for free and under the supervision of a trusted educator. In exchange for content, savvy instructors will insist that professionals give students direct evaluation and feedback. They may also ask media professionals to lead a classroom discussion or invite students into the workplace. It is a relationship from which both businesses and schools benefit. Businesses get free labor and potential recruits; students are almost guaranteed to learn from the exchange—and have something to show for it in their portfolios.

Two good examples of the project-management mentality and how it affects TMS Campus are playing themselves out in different ways at the University of North Carolina, at Chapel Hill's School of Journalism and Mass Communication.

The first is associate dean Jan Yopp's reporting class. At the beginning of the fall 1999 semester, Yopp worked with TMS Campus to develop a topic for her students to explore. She chose "dating on college campuses" and allowed students to devise a list of stories that would be suitable for a series to be distributed to TMS Campus' clients the following spring. The students were also encouraged to take photographs to support stories, devise info-graphics, and suggest ways to integrate audio and video into their coverage. At the end of the semester, Yopp graded the students' work and submitted it to TMS Campus. From there, the news organization edited the work and provided students with more direct feedback before distributing the content. Students who contributed to the project had published work to show for it later.

The second example is the UNC journalism school's independent study elective, supervised by senior associate dean Tom Bowers. During the fall 1999 semester, Bowers assigned four journalism students, who wanted to sharpen their writing and reporting skills, to a semester of TMS Campus's journalism training program. The students wrote several news items of varying length, completed exercises in copyediting, and conducted research using the Internet. Each week, the students filed notes via e-mail to let Bowers and TMS know what they had learned and to ask questions about some of the work-related issues they had encountered. My responsibility was to respond each week with e-mail notes or telephone calls to address their observations and concerns.

At the end of the semester, we agreed that ours had been a wonderfully productive working relationship—even though I was working hundreds of miles away from UNC. TMS Campus staff were able to shift more entry-level, everyday tasks to students who needed to learn basic journalism skills.

In exchange for promising some oversight and teaching, the company received much-needed help, and the students received course credit and valuable work experience. While this example comes from a four-year institution, the lessons learned are important for, and applicable to, just about any media course.

Help Students Look for Publishing Opportunities Beyond Campus

We have already established that many Web sites need content and are happy to accept work from freelance contributors. Granted, the pay is usually paltry—if anything at all—but the experience is valuable and the deadline pressures are real.

But just where are some of these Web publishing opportunities? Finding them, said Elise Lanoue, executive producer of www.thepavement.com, is simple, once a student identifies his or her interests.

"The Web is about building community," she said during our interview. "The best way to become a contributing writer or editor is to find a community that's right for you and start adding your voice to it. Contributing for free will get you invited to host a message board, and that will get you invited to write a column or freelance stories for pay. That's the way editors get to know contributors."

Thepavement.com is a good example of a community-building Web site that depends heavily on students' perspectives. Besides being a for-profit organization, its aim is to help young journalists establish their careers, manage their finances, find apartments, and buy cars. Lanoue said that she and her staff are constantly looking for writers who can deliver first-person, blow-by-blow accounts of their job searches or unusual work experiences—which the average community-college student is sure to know plenty about.

Another interesting Web site is www.content-exchange.com, billed as "the digital marketplace for on-line content creators and publishers." Managed in part by renowned Internet columnist and publisher Steve Outing, the site matches "content producers"—such as editors, graphic designers, interactive tool developers, photographers, proofreaders, researchers, writers and video specialists—with "publishing venues." Two primary databases drive the site; one allows Web publishers to seek content providers, and the other does the opposite.

When it comes to publishing opportunities for students, I would be remiss in not mentioning TMS Campus again, because it is always looking for student journalists to join its ranks—whether as an extracurricular activity or for independent study credit. TMS and similar organizations want and need more participation from students at community colleges, which we know face many issues far different from those of traditional, four-year institutions.

Make Sure Your Campus's Student Newspaper Has an On-Line Edition

Colleges without an on-line edition of the campus newspaper are doing students a great disservice. In the professional world, reporters are increasingly asked to file stories for both hard copy and Web editions and to understand how to adapt their work to suit both. It is important for both college public relations professions to understand that print newspapers and on-line newspapers are very different!

On-line editions provide better training for students planning to enter today's newsrooms (especially if the campus's print newspaper comes out only once or twice a week, or, even worse, once or twice a month) by giving them plenty of opportunities to cover breaking news. Save the analysis for the hard copy edition that will come out later.

An on-line edition would also encourage more students to join the newspaper staff and would, in the process, foster a more interdisciplinary environment, much like the one found in many professional newsrooms. Graphic designers, computer programmers, interactive tool developers—they all play an important role in the production of a newspaper for the Web.

In addition, an on-line newspaper is not bound to the same space constraints as its print brethren. That, of course, frees photographers and writers to provide more in-depth coverage on any number of topics.

Create an On-Line Campus News Operation

Any communications department that fancies itself "modern" should be training young journalists to enter what is purely new media.

To do so, instructors would be wise to help establish on-line campus news organizations that would be strongly allied with, but not subservient to, student newspapers and broadcast stations. After all, the Internet truly is a medium unto itself.

The different media should be encouraged to join forces—allowing shared use of content, cross-promotional efforts, and some package deals for ad sales.

While the on-line news organization might feature some stories from the student newspaper, or sound and video clips from the student broadcast stations, its focus should be on generating original content.

In a column for *Editor and Publisher Interactive,* Steve Outing writes:

> It shouldn't be a newspaper online, although it may have some elements of an online paper. The campus Web operation can take a cue from what professional news/information Web sites have done, such as: creating a campus business directory; hosting an online relationships/dating service; accepting online classified ads (perhaps in competition with the student newspaper); providing a campus/city entertainment guide and calendar; designing and hosting Web sites for student groups, etc. Obviously, some of these ideas are not exactly "journalism." But new media is not just about journalism, and students should be encouraged to build new interactive services—and test out their entrepreneurial skills as well as their communications abilities.

There is no reason for communications departments to shoulder the responsibility—or cost—of creating such a Web organization alone. An on-line campus news operation would be far more dynamic if it were treated with an interdisciplinary approach. Students interested in content production could work with computer science students interested in building Web sites, with marketing students interested in promoting them, and with business students interested in financing them.

Sounds as if it would be a great class.

Reference

Outing, S. *Editor and Publisher Interactive*, Aug. 27, 1999.

CHRISTINE TATUM is a reporter for Tribune Media Services, a division of the Tribune Company in Chicago. She covers national issues and trends in higher education and directs the TMS Campus Correspondents Program, a national network of student reporters, photographers, cartoonists, and graphic artists (www.tmscampus.com).

10

Community colleges are not the only institutions making use of the World Wide Web.

Your Site or Mine? Courting the Press Along the Information Superhighway

Clifton Truman Daniel

The first college news item I managed to pitch successfully to the *Chicago Tribune*—a nice blurb about Truman College students raising money for Honduran flood victims—did not wind up in that newspaper at all. It ended up on the Internet.

My reaction at the time was "Great, I got a story out" but also "Hey, why didn't I get it in the *real* paper? Who is going to see this?"

Well, more people than you can shake a stick at, probably. Most newspapers and other media outlets have electronic versions of their daily, weekly, and monthly content. Through those Web sites, public relations professionals at community colleges can reach media contacts faster and with more up-to-date information than they can through traditional means. Public relations professionals can also save reams of fax paper and fudge on deadlines, if needed. All it takes is etiquette and openness to new ideas.

Community Colleges

There is no doubt that all institutions of higher education have benefited from resources and services available to them through the Internet. It is becoming more common for two-year colleges across the United States to have a Web site posted on the Internet. Colleges without their own "on-ramp" to the Information Superhighway are fewer and farther between. Maricopa Community College sponsors a searchable Web site that provides a comprehensive list of community college Web sites in the United States, Canada, and elsewhere around the world. The interface to the index allows

All individuals quoted in this chapter were interviewed in March 2000.

you to search alphabetically (by the first letter of the college's name), geographically (by the country/state/province), or by keywords in the college name, location, or Web address (http://www.mcli.dist.maricopa.edu/cc/index.htm).

There is real evidence that a presence on the Web is a great way to get the word out about a college. Denise Wilkin, assistant dean for institutional advancement at Harold Washington College, a campus of City Colleges of Chicago, has received visits, or "hits," on her college's Web site from as far away as Italy. That particular hit, for example, came from a former student serving in the U.S. military, who had graduated from one of Harold Washington's distance learning programs. He was reacting to Harold Washington College's Web site posting of the program's alumni newsletter.

More often, though, Wilkin uses the Web for audiences closer to home. "We use the Web to get our stuff out," she said. "I submit press releases and stories of interest . . . anything that has to do with advancing the institution. The issue is that our students are all over the place. They're all over the city."

Truman College has also had great success in using the Web to reach potential students not only in our own back yard but also across the nation and around the world. According to Joy Walker, Truman College's assistant dean of instructional technology, Truman's Web site receives approximately eight thousand hits each month. The number of first-time visitors to the college's site increased from twenty-eight hundred in November 1999 to thirty-eight hundred in January 2000. In addition, the Truman Web site has been visited by many countries outside the United States, including Japan, Bosnia, Brazil, Chile, Colombia, Sweden, the United Arab Emirates, and the United Kingdom.

Newspapers

"Quite frankly, the Web is providing a much larger potential readership," said Christine Tatum—a contributor to this issue and manager of Tribune Media Services Campus, and the person who accepted my news item on Truman College students helping Honduran flood victims. "Anybody around the world can spot it."

TMS Campus is a *Tribune*-owned, Web-based wire service that is used and contributed to by college newspapers across the country. Truman College's Honduras item was eventually picked up by several college newspapers around the country, showcasing an essential and positive trait about Truman College, which is that faculty, staff, and students put an emphasis on community service.

Two of the local weeklies—*Lerner Newspapers* and *Inside Publications*—produce good on-line versions of their papers. *Inside* will accept copy almost verbatim and at any time. If you miss the deadline for the paper itself, you can always get your item into the "e-paper."

"We're your friendly neighborhood newspaper," said Publisher Ron Roenigk. "In fact, I even took the door off my office. It doesn't even exist anymore. That's our gig, is to be accessible."

Inside's goal is to become both a community bulletin board and a daily news service, both of which serve Truman College and other two-year colleges in the metropolitan region. The on-line version of their paper is the ideal place to post upcoming events as well as news stories.

"The on-line news hole is limitless, really," Roenigk said. "Notices of special events, festivals, classes, block club meetings, PTA meetings, and church group meetings are all welcome." He added, "As long as we can trust you, we'll copy it right over to the news page, guaranteed. We would like to be all things to all people. If you're in our coverage area and you're having a bake sale, well, that should be in there. Potentially, it's the only chance to get total market coverage."

Though larger papers like the *Chicago Tribune* and the *Chicago Sun-Times* are not as all-embracing as *Inside* and other community papers, their reporters more and more often deal electronically with public relations officials.

"Their preferred order of receipt used to be U.S. mail, phone, then fax," said Ronan Roche of June Rosner Public Relations, in Chicago, which contracts with Truman College and the other six campuses of City Colleges of Chicago. "Now, it's e-mail, fax, phone and U.S. mail, so the electronic has taken over the actual contact."

Reporters, who spend hours chained to their computers when they're not out on the street, use the Internet to work faster and sort through the reams of information that comes their way.

"The use of attached files and documents has speeded up the process of pitching a product or press release enormously," Roche said. "There's no physically searching for the fax machine. It's just click on, read, and reply through the forward button."

A college public relations director or Webmaster can make a reporter's job even easier by posting press releases on the Web site, under a special button labeled "Press Room" or something similar.

"Just take all your press releases and put them there," said Tom Ciesielka, also of Rosner Public Relations.

If a news story is ongoing—say, it's about the funding and construction of a new building—Ciesielka suggested not just updating one release, but posting all past releases, plus anything else you think might be helpful or informative.

"They can go back and see past releases," he said. "Give them a research tool."

Building Relationships

Take the time to get to know not only the higher education reporter, but also the Web staff—and give them respect as well.

"It pays off to introduce yourself to the on-line editor as well as the editor of the traditional newspaper," the *Tribune's* Tatum said. "Don't assume that they are one and the same person."

Call first. "I hate unsolicited e-mail," Tatum said. "I feel as if it is a back-door way of getting something into my face, and I am already a very busy person." Reporters are wary of unsolicited e-mails because they sometimes harbor computer viruses.

Make e-mail pitches short and sweet. "Bullets are OK," Tatum said. "I need it fast and I do not have time to read a book report."

When sending an e-mail with text taken from the Web, strip off the HTML coding so the reporter doesn't have to deal with a ten-page e-mail, nine pages of which is code. Also, if you are sending the information to more than one person, use the "blind cc" function. Reporters prefer not to have their e-mail addresses posted for everyone to see.

Better yet, e-mail a short note with a link to your Web site. That way, the reporter knows what you would like her to see and she can look at it when she has time, Tatum said.

The University of Cincinnati publishes a weekly on-line press briefing shot with punchy "teasers" to topics of interest and lists of instructors' names and e-mail addresses. When a reporter finds something of interest to him, he can pull up more information from the Web site, or call or e-mail an instructor.

Always follow an e-mail with a personal call. "Waiting for me to call you is not a smart thing," Tatum said. "You are going to want to follow up your e-mail with a call to me. And that, of course, I think is reasonable."

Suggestions for Television and Radio

In the end, one can take comfort in the fact that even if you or your institution does not use the Web on a daily basis, news from your college—whether it is disseminated through newspapers, radio, or television—may wind up on it anyway. If you manage to secure a television interview for a dean, for example, the station is likely to use the audio portion on radio (if it owns radio station), and then archive the video clips on the Web.

"See who has this flow-down effect to help maximize your communications," Ciesielka said. "You do one thing where you get three results."

Conclusion

The possibilities for promoting your college through the Internet are nearly limitless, not to mention exciting. News from the college can be delivered faster to more people than ever before, and will be more up to date. The Web will also prove to be a superior marketing tool as community colleges begin to collect more and better data on the people who are most interested in and can benefit most from their services.

Pay close attention to your Web pages and make them as interesting and as cutting-edge as possible, both as advertisement for the college and its programs and as a platform for working with members of the media. Build relationships not only with a newspaper's print editors, but with its electronic editors as well. Use the styles and methods that reporters prefer, and enjoy the fact that you can communicate faster and more accurately through the Internet. Encourage both students and staff with an interest in the Web to pursue it. You never know when you will come up with a Webmaster who can help you transform your Web page from something that you have simply because everyone else does, into a truly effective marketing and public relations tool.

CLIFTON TRUMAN DANIEL is the director of public relations at Harry S Truman College, one of the City Colleges of Chicago.

11

This annotated bibliography presents recent ERIC documents that provide insight into the public perception of community colleges, the potential influence of the media on public opinion regarding community colleges, institutional relations with the media, and the role that Web pages play in strategic marketing.

Sources and Information: Media Relations in Community Colleges

Barbara Tobolowsky

Understanding public perceptions of community colleges and using that knowledge to shape marketing campaigns that inform and publicize the work of community colleges has become a primary goal of campus public relations officers. Media sources, from newspapers to the World Wide Web, play a significant role in communicating those achievements to the public as well as providing interdepartmental communication.

The following publications reflect the current ERIC literature on public perceptions of community colleges and institutional relationships with the media. They also offer numerous case studies of specific institutions that use multiple forms of media, including the Web, for providing information to the public as well as serving as an internal communications device. Most ERIC documents (publications with ED numbers) can be viewed on microfiche at over nine hundred libraries worldwide. In addition, most may be ordered on microfiche or on paper from the ERIC Document Reproduction Service (EDRS) by calling (800) 443-ERIC. Journal articles are not available from EDRS, but they can be acquired through regular library channels or purchased from the University Microfilm International Articles Clearinghouse at (800) 521-0600, extension 533.

General Articles

These articles provide insight into the potential influence of the media as well as public perceptions of community colleges.

Getskow, V. A. "Community College: Impressions and Images Gained Through Publications." Master's research paper, University of California, Los Angeles, 1996. (ED 400 000)

The community college movement has been well documented since the organization of the first junior colleges. This documentation has been maintained by six groups: (1) scholars and professors, (2) the popular media, (3) institutional research, (4) state agencies, (5) faculty organizations, and (6) national organizations. Written by recognized experts in the field, this research is generally influential, but is usually published in scholarly journals with limited readerships. In contrast, newspapers and magazines produced by the popular media have the potential for vast readership, which makes them the most influential category of documents.

Absher, K., and Crawford, G. "Marketing the Community College Starts with Understanding Students' Perspectives." *Community College Review,* 1996, 23(4), 59–67. (EJ 524 868)

This article examines variables taken into account by community college students in choosing a college—such as quality of education, faculty, cost, physical attractiveness, and accessibility—and argues that increased competition for students means that colleges must employ marketing strategies to attract individuals to their institutions. Research confirms that colleges "have distinguishable images"; therefore, marketing strategies can be developed focusing on these distinguishing traits. Absher and Crawford discuss the use of selection factors as market segmentation tools and identify five principal market segments, based on student classifications of important variables:

- The "practical-minded" are concerned with reputation, quality of education, and cost issues.
- "Advice seekers" follow the advice of high school counselors and parents.
- "Joe College" responds to advertising and published materials.
- "Goodtimers" are attracted to social activities offered at the school.
- "Warm friendlies" are concerned with school size, location, and physical attractiveness.

Community college administrators must use their knowledge of the student market to plan their communication efforts to attract and maintain students.

Frederick Community College. *Frederick County Community Perception Survey: Planning, Research and Evaluation at Frederick Community College, Md.* Frederick, Md.: Frederick Community College, 1997. (ED 421 187)

In 1997, Frederick Community College (FCC) in Maryland conducted a telephone survey of a random sample of 466 Frederick County residents to identify their perceptions of the college. In particular, the survey examined Frederick County residents' image of FCC, their level of awareness of services and programs offered by FCC, and the types of services that affected their enrollment decisions. All the residents interviewed were at least eighteen years of age. Findings from 348 respondents, whose ages ranged between eighteen and fifty-nine years of age, were as follows:

- Eighty-five percent of county residents interviewed rated FCC's reputation as "good" or "very good."
- Of all the county residents attending any college in the past two years, 62 percent attended FCC.
- Half of those interviewed were not aware of FCC's programs for children.
- Although 70 percent rated the variety of courses as good or very good, only 55 percent rated FCC course offerings as being relevant to the world of work.
- Seventy percent rated FCC as affordable.
- Three out of four respondents had a personal computer in their home and nearly half reported having access to the Internet.

Graphs of responses from residents eighteen to fifty-nine years old, responses by age and gender, and responses from residents at least sixty years of age are included.

Media Relations

These documents discuss specific uses of media by community colleges to benefit the college including increasing enrollment, aiding fundraising, and persuading voters to support taxes that would help local community colleges. The types of media range from low-tech efforts such as newsletters to more sophisticated and costly approaches like public service announcements aired on television.

Golden, S. "The Media and Your Message: Getting the Coverage You Want." *Community College Journal,* 1992, *63*(3), 48–52. (EJ 451 975)
    Mass media outlets reach a large, diverse audience and give "credibility far beyond what an ad or brochure can achieve" (p. 48). This article discusses how public affairs staff should work with the media to get good coverage and recounts how several community colleges reaped public relations successes through positive media coverage. It also offers examples of award-winning communications efforts. For example, Cuyahoga Community College in Cleveland, Ohio, devised a campaign featuring successful alumni in a series of press conferences and public service announcements produced for area TV stations, combined with radio pitches conducted by both public affairs staff and students. In 1991 they received the Paragon Award for this outstanding media effort that succeeded in convincing voters to support a tax levy.

Kell, C. A. "Building Public Support Through the Media." *Trustee Quarterly,* 1997, *4*. (ED 415 937)
    The author advises community college administrators that "newspapers, radio, and television are the most effective and least costly ways to get your name and issues before a wide audience" (p. 3). She goes on to offer numerous tips on how to deal with reporters—from being accessible to

being concise. This issue of the journal focuses on advocacy for access and the use of media.

Miller, L., and Fuchcar, P. "It's Perfect for You: The 1994 Recruitment Effort of Chattanooga State Technical Community College." Paper presented at the Annual International Conference of the National Institute for Staff and Organizational Development on Teaching Excellence and Conference of Administrators, Austin, Tex., May 21–24, 1995. (ED 388 354)

In 1993, Chattanooga State Technical Community College (CSTCC) in Tennessee experienced its first drop in enrollment in seven years. In an effort to increase enrollment the CSTCC adopted a new approach to marketing. External factors that indicated a potential further decline in enrollment were examined and a four-part strategy that included research, program development, outreach, and promotion was implemented to respond to the changing external forces. With respect to promotional activities, CSTCC offset the declines in available resources by using electronic and print media advertising, outdoor display advertising, an information center at the shopping mall, and a cable television "documercial" focusing on CSTCC's program areas, as well as information on registration and financial aid. The college managed to achieve its goals of maintaining the level of enrolled credits and increasing previous enrollment rates for the fall 1994 semester. CSTCC's success is particularly noteworthy because another community college nearby had almost a 10 percent decline in enrollment. CSTCC attributed its success to this marketing campaign.

McCabe, R. H. *Project Reinvest: Invest in America's Future by Reinvesting in America's Community Colleges.* Mission Viejo, Calif.: League for Innovation in the Community College, 1995. (ED 384 368)

To raise the level of funding for the nation's community colleges, Project Reinvest was created to help colleges communicate both their role in solving the nation's problems and the importance of adequate funding for higher education. Specifically, the project seeks to encourage colleges' participation in efforts to develop a genuine understanding of their institutions and to gain strong local support, and to provide information and assistance for colleges developing fundraising campaigns. This article discusses a number of future efforts that are a part of the plan. For example, to assist fundraising efforts at the national level, articles on the colleges will be prepared for such periodicals as flight magazines, business-oriented magazines, and general circulation publications. In addition, efforts will be coordinated with local institutions, the American Association of Community Colleges, and the League for Innovation in the Community College to increase visibility through newspaper articles and radio and television presentations. To aid efforts at the local level, packages of support material will be prepared for use by local colleges, including guides to building local support, developing private fundraising, and bringing local campaigns to the state level. Participating institutions will be enrolled through their presidents in a project information interchange and networking system managed by the project director. Finally, the director will also conduct site visits to help institutions organize or make community presentations.

Pappas, R. J. (ed.). *Strategic Marketing for Presidents*. Washington, D.C.: American Association of Community Colleges, 1994. (ED 368 417)

Designed to inform the marketing efforts of community college presidents, this document describes the importance of marketing, presents a targeted approach, and outlines the specific roles and skills needed by the college's president to ensure successful efforts and effective institutions. The first chapter, "Developing a Marketing-Strategic Plan," by Richard J. Pappas and M. Richard Shaink, introduces marketing principles and describes ten steps for developing a marketing plan in a community college. In Chapter Five, "The President's Role in Public Relations," Beverly S. Simone outlines the important role the president plays in establishing a good working relationship with the media. She advises presidents to meet with editorial boards and explain the college's mission and "its role in strengthening the community" (p. 73). She also says that presidents should be accessible to the media, be accurate and concise when offering information, and understand when to use the media and when it is best to remain silent. She brings up an example of an appropriate presidential "salary adjustment" that brought the college negative publicity (p. 74). Rather than address this issue to the press, Simone advises silence, realizing that drawing attention to the incident will just further increase the public's ire.

Janke, W., and Kelly, G. *Developing a More Effective Recruitment and Retention Model*. Milwaukee, Wis.: Milwaukee Area Technical College, 1992. (ED 362 735)

The purpose of the project was to develop a model for more effective recruitment and retention of people of color in the Associate Degree in Interior Design and Diploma in Interior Design Assistant programs at Milwaukee Area Technical College (MATC) in Wisconsin. During stage one, individuals in MATC's student development and high school relations departments, as well as the Milwaukee Public Schools resource people, were interviewed to determine strategies for recruiting high school students. After developing an understanding of the targeted population, several recommendations were made as to how to attract students to this program, and a marketing plan was devised. One of the primary marketing efforts was a video produced to highlight interior design careers, consisting of interviews with six interior designers and features on current students' experiences.

Nazzaro, J. P. "Community College Alumni: Partners in Resource Development." Paper presented at the Junior and Community College Institute's Alumni Development Workshop, Washington, D.C., 1992. (ED 358 904)

The County College of Morris (CCM) in Randolph, New Jersey, was established in 1968, and over twenty thousand students have received degrees or certificates from the college since its founding. In an effort to improve alumni involvement, a new alumni program was established under the Division of College Advancement, and a part-time alumni director was hired. To promote involvement in the new alumni association, CCM implemented a plan to feature alumni as "community stars," placing them in public fundraising efforts. An institutional image marketing campaign was also developed and five key alumni were chosen to be featured spokespersons for the college in all advertising for a given period. The selected alumni appeared in advertising media that included billboards, newspapers, magazines, cable television, and radio spots. The campaign resulted in a successful fundraising drive. However, CCM administrators saw even more benefits from the campaign. They believe that it "increased our visibility, enhanced our image," and gave "institutional pride to current students" (p. 8).

Rothlisberg, A. P. "Sharing the Good News: A Rural Approach to Publicizing Community College Library Services." Holbrook, Ariz.: Northland Pioneer College, 1992. (ED 344 613). For related papers, see ED 346 861, ED 332 706, ED 335 029, and ED 335 039.

The Northland Pioneer College (NPC) library staff has developed a media blitz strategy to publicize its services in rural Arizona. This strategy regularly draws on a database of newspapers, radio stations, and cable television outlets in the area. Each week a different public service announcement is developed and sent out to agencies on the database. Announcements range from different types of information provided at the college libraries to the availability of state and federal tax forms. The release material is never more than a page long and is printed on college stationery. The school began to see cable companies using library material when discussing NPC and they noted that many of their announcements found their way into the rural newspapers and led to follow-up pieces on the local radio. The college was able to measure increased library usage and noticed that people were asking about services that were highlighted in the press releases, leading them to credit the publicity approach for the increases.

Reed, A. *Systemwide Communications Plan and Priorities.* Sacramento: California Community Colleges, Office of the Chancellor. Agenda item at the meeting of the board of governors of the California Community Colleges, Nov. 14–15, 1991. (ED 337 223)

The board of governors of the California Community Colleges has repeatedly identified the strengthening of communication as a key component for developing the California Community Colleges (CCC) as a system. The genesis of communication planning, activities, and priorities took place in 1989 with the Burson-Marsteller Communications Action Plan. The action plan, generated through a statewide survey and evaluation of the public image of the CCC, outlines the priorities for strengthening the communications activities of the CCC with regard to public understanding of the system. Each year, the CCC Foundation has funded at least one priority activity from the action plan. Key activities that have been completed include the State Chancellor's Hour monthly public affairs show, the quarterly *Impact* newsletter, and a system video. Other major new initiatives are being considered for the future, including the development of a statewide community college newspaper and increased national media exposure in conjunction with the CCC's Commission on Innovation. The Burson-Marsteller Communications review, the Action Plan, and a division work plan aligned to the available funding for projects are attached.

Web Pages Playing a Media Role

With the popularization of the Internet in recent years, community colleges have turned to the Web to help publicize their campus to the public and prospective students as well as help provide interdepartmental communication.

McCollum, K. "Colleges Revamp Web Pages with Professional Help." *Chronicle of Higher Education,* July 16, 1999. p. A25.
    The Web site has become a key element in colleges' and universities' marketing strategies. It communicates to key constituents, students, faculty members, staff members, and the public. Web pages are important to convey a range of information about the school—from stating institutional missions to providing faculty e-mail addresses to helping students make textbook purchases. Because the college Web page has become so significant in representing the school to prospective students and others, professional design firms have cropped up to create visually interesting sites that are also user-friendly.

Carr, L. *Service Learning Content on the Internet: How Are Community Colleges Advertising?* 1999. (ED 428 782)
    This study examines how eleven community colleges present and promote their service learning courses via the Internet. Of particular interest to this study are the following seven features of on-line presentations: (1) how detailed and developed the Web site is and the amount of information provided; (2) whether the Web site provides student and faculty responses to service learning participation; (3) what the Web site emphasizes (for example, student leadership, volunteerism, or community service); (4) inclusion of community partnerships; (5) contracts or learning agreements; (6) program evaluation; and (7) coursework and other sample information.

Boettcher, S., and Schwartz, R. "Team-Building Through Technology: Using a Newsletter or a Web Site to Energize Your Department." *Walking the*

Tightrope: The Balance Between Innovation and Leadership. Proceedings of the Annual International Conference of the Chair Academy, Reno, Nev., Feb. 12–15, 1997. (ED 407 026)

One of the most difficult problems facing department chairs is one of inspiring a shared vision of the department, especially among part-time faculty. A departmental forum—or a central means of communication that is regularly updated and widely accessible—can be useful in fostering teamwork and a shared vision. Two popular formats for forums are newsletters and Web pages. In developing a forum, it is essential that basic policy issues be resolved beforehand—including the forum's purpose and audience, what content will be appropriate, the format, methods for ensuring faculty participation, and goals, with respect to how ambitious the project will be. In planning a text-based newsletter, key strategies include: combining graphics with text to make the publications visually engaging; combining news with feature stories; designing catchy nameplates, mastheads, and headlines; and producing occasional special issues. The Web is a useful tool for providing graphics and text as well as hypertext links to other resources. To create a Web-based forum, a Web browser, a simple text editor, and knowledge of basic hypertext markup language (HTML) codes are required.

Barbara Tobolowsky is in the doctoral program in higher education and organizational change at the University of California, Los Angeles.

INDEX

Back Issue/Subscription Order Form

Copy or detach and send to:
Jossey-Bass Inc., 350 Sansome Street, San Francisco CA 94104-1342

Call or fax toll free!
Phone 888-378-2537 6AM-5PM PST; Fax 800-605-2665

Back issues: Please send me the following issues at $25 each
(Important: please include series initials and issue number, such as CC90)

1. CC _____

_____

$ _____ Total for single issues

$ _____ Shipping charges (for single issues *only;* subscriptions are exempt
from shipping charges): Up to $30, add $5^{50} • $30^{01}–$50, add $6^{50}
$50^{01}–$75, add $8 • $75^{01}–$100, add $10 • $100^{01}–$150, add $12
Over $150, call for shipping charge

Subscriptions Please ❑ start ❑ renew my subscription to *New Directions
for Community Colleges* for the year ___ at the following rate:

U.S.:	❑ Individual $60	❑ Institutional $107
Canada:	❑ Individual $85	❑ Institutional $132
All Others:	❑ Individual $90	❑ Institutional $137

NOTE: Subscriptions are quarterly, and are for the calendar year only.
Subscriptions begin with the Spring issue of the year indicated above.

$ _____ Total single issues and subscriptions (Add appropriate sales tax for
your state for single issue orders. No sales tax for U.S. subscriptions.
Canadaian residents, add GST for subscriptions and single issues.)

❑ Payment enclosed (U.S. check or money order only)
❑ VISA, MC, AmEx, Discover Card #_____ Exp. date_____

Signature _____ Day phone _____
❑ Bill me (U.S. institutional orders only. Purchase order required)
Purchase order #_____

Federal Tax ID 13559 3032   GST 89102-8052

Name _____

Address _____

_____

Phone_____ E-mail _____

For more information about Jossey-Bass, visit our Web site at:
www.josseybass.com   **PRIORITY CODE = ND1**